Business Process Management with JBoss jBPM

A Practical Guide for Business Analysts

Develop business process models for implementation in a business process management system

Matt Cumberlidge

PUBLISHING

BIRMINGHAM - MUMBAI

Business Process Management with JBoss jBPM

A Practical Guide for Business Analysts

First published: July 2007

Production Reference: 1190707

Published by Packt Publishing Ltd.
32 Lincoln Road
Olton
Birmingham, B27 6PA, UK.

ISBN 978-1-847192-36-3

www.packtpub.com

Cover Image by Vinayak Chittar (vinayak.chittar@gmail.com)

Credits

Author
Matt Cumberlidge

Reviewers
Diego Naya Lazo
Dr. David Franklin
Sebastien Michea

Senior Acquisition Editor
David Barnes

Development Editor
Nikhil Bangera

Technical Editor
Ajay S

Project Manager
Abhijeet Deobhakta

Editorial Manager
Dipali Chittar

Project Coordinator
Sagara Naik

Indexer
Bhushan Pangaonkar

Proofreader
Chris Smith

Production Coordinator
Manjiri Nadkarni

Cover Designer
Shantanu Zagade

About the Author

Matt Cumberlidge is a business analyst working for a world leading FTSE 100 provider of information-driven services and solutions based in Oxford, UK. In this role, Matt has undertaken a very wide range of projects, but the common theme running throughout is that of business process. Over the last year or so Matt has extended his core capabilities in business process analysis and re-engineering into the realm of business process management and in particular an investigation of the JBoss jBPM implementation. Matt is delighted to be able to share his experiences and ideas about this exciting technology with a wider audience through the publication of this book.

I'd like to thank my wife, Cathy, for understanding why I wasn't always available to do my share of the housework while I was writing this book and for feeding the cats, who would otherwise surely have died of hunger. I'd like to thank Phil Wilkins from SeeWhy for going way beyond the call of duty in helping me. I'd like to thank my publishers, Packt, and in particular Dave Barnes for his encouragement. Lastly, I'd like to thank and pay tribute to the contributors to the JBoss jBPM community who have built a fantastic product that it was fun for me to write about.

About the Reviewers

Diego Naya Lazo is a Chief Enterprise Architect living in Buenos Aires, Argentina. He currently works for Argentina's biggest healthcare provider and has more than 10 years of experience in the IT industry. He participated in several projects as a hands-on software architect and performed the technical lead role in many companies. His interest in computer programming began with his desire to create the most vivid 3D animations as a graphic designer at the age of 15.

Dr David Franklin is an experienced hands-on software architect with more than 20 years experience with leading-edge companies and technologies.

Sebastien Michea is a J2EE software architect at Manaty (`www.manaty.net`).

After a PhD in Mathematical Physics at Université de Bourgogne (Dijon, France), he studied Quantum Statistical systems in Yonsei university (Seoul). Programming with Java since its first version, he joined Cap Gemini Telecom in Paris as a Java developer. He then worked at PSU (State College, USA) as a Lecturer and Researcher in the Computer Science and Mathematics department and simultaneously developed a trading system based on non-linear correlations.

In 2006 he founded Manaty, an open-source IT company which is closer to a freelancer community than a traditional company that create software using cutting-edge technologies like EJB3, Flex, and.NET.

His main areas of interest are software design, science, linguistic, and cooking.

Table of contents

Preface

This book shows business analysts how to model business processes in JBoss jBPM and use these models to generate a fully-functioning workflow application. It shows how business analysts can use the tools to build a solution without the need for Java coding expertise. It also introduces more advanced functionality that can be implemented by Java developers in partnership with the Business Analyst.

This book takes a practical approach, with step-by-step instructions for business process management, model creation, and implementation. It uses a typical BPM project lifecycle case study to explore and explain the process in a realistic situation.

What this book covers

Chapter 1 discusses the background from which BPM has emerged, and how BPM fits into the wider scheme of enterprise application development. We define what BPM means for us, and look at the business scenarios where BPM is the right solution. Also, we introduce our suggested BPM project lifecycle, and see the tools that we'll put together as our open source-based BPM suite.

Chapter 2 covers all the major tools in the process analyst's kit bag, with a view to creating a deep understanding of the process we are seeking to systematize in our BPMS.

Chapter 3 covers the software installations—Java, the JBoss application server, the jBPM engine, and the jBPM Designer. Also, we take a look at the fundamental concepts that underpin JBoss jBPM and put these concepts into practice by building our first process definition for our proof-of-concept system.

Chapter 4 covers building the user interface that our proof-of-concept testers will use to interact with the process definition that we built in the previous chapter.

Chapter 5 covers putting the jBPM system on a server so our proof-of-concept testers can bash their test data into it and give us feedback on what they think. Also, how we can allow managers to prioritize tasks by design and on the fly. Most complicated of all, we see how our system can be integrated with other applications, both in house and external.

Chapter 6 looks at how we judge when we are ready to start planning to go live and also covers the essentials we need to consider when building an implementation plan. We show how the web console can be customized according to your own branding and we see how we can swap the default jBPM database for a more robust, enterprise-ready database server. We will also integrate and put to use the SeeWhy Business Activity Monitoring solution.

Chapter 7 covers how to assess our project and perform process analysis and ongoing improvement. We also put together business process documentation, and present ideas for further development of our BPM system.

What you need for this book

You will need access to an installation of the JBoss jBPM engine and the JBoss application server, along with the JBoss jBPM designer. There is a walk-through on how to install them in Chapter 3 of this book.

JBoss jBPM requires a working installation of the latest version of Java and a Java utility called Ant. Details about how to download, install, and configure them are given in Chapter 3 of this book.

You'll also need access to a MySQL installation in order to do some of the more complex pieces

Conventions

In this book, you will find a number of styles of text that distinguish between different kinds of information. Here are some examples of these styles, and an explanation of their meaning.

There are three styles for code. Code words in text are shown as follows: "We can include other contexts through the use of the `include` directive."

A block of code will be set as follows:

```
<html xmlns="http://www.w3.org/1999/xhtml"
      xmlns:ui="http://java.sun.com/jsf/facelets"
      xmlns:c="http://java.sun.com/jstl/core"
      xmlns:h="http://java.sun.com/jsf/html"
      xmlns:f="http://java.sun.com/jsf/core"
```

When we wish to draw your attention to a particular part of a code block, the relevant lines or items will be made bold:

```
<task name="Hold auditions" swimlane="Talent scout" priority="1">
    <controller>
        <variable name="audDate" access="read,write,required"
                                    mapped-name="Audition
```

New terms and **important words** are introduced in a bold-type font. Words that you see on the screen, in menus or dialog boxes for example, appear in our text like this: "clicking the **Next** button moves you to the next screen".

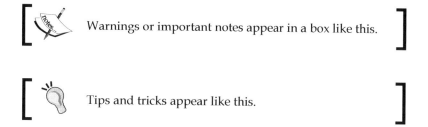

Warnings or important notes appear in a box like this.

Tips and tricks appear like this.

Reader feedback

Feedback from our readers is always welcome. Let us know what you think about this book, what you liked or may have disliked. Reader feedback is important for us to develop titles that you really get the most out of.

To send us general feedback, simply drop an email to feedback@packtpub.com, making sure to mention the book title in the subject of your message.

If there is a book that you need and would like to see us publish, please send us a note in the **SUGGEST A TITLE** form on www.packtpub.com or email suggest@packtpub.com.

If there is a topic that you have expertise in and you are interested in either writing or contributing to a book, see our author guide on www.packtpub.com/authors.

Customer support

Now that you are the proud owner of a Packt book, we have a number of things to help you to get the most from your purchase.

Downloading the example code for the book

Visit http://www.packtpub.com/support, and select this book from the list of titles to download any example code or extra resources for this book. The files available for download will then be displayed.

 The downloadable files contain instructions on how to use them.

Errata

Although we have taken every care to ensure the accuracy of our contents, mistakes do happen. If you find a mistake in one of our books—maybe a mistake in text or code—we would be grateful if you would report this to us. By doing this you can save other readers from frustration, and help to improve subsequent versions of this book. If you find any errata, report them by visiting http://www.packtpub.com/support, selecting your book, clicking on the **Submit Errata** link, and entering the details of your errata. Once your errata are verified, your submission will be accepted and the errata added to the list of existing errata. The existing errata can be viewed by selecting your title from http://www.packtpub.com/support.

Questions

You can contact us at questions@packtpub.com if you are having a problem with some aspect of the book, and we will do our best to address it.

1
Introduction

Business Process Management is one of the hottest topics in the fast-moving world of business analysis and enterprise application development. Yet, it is curiously difficult to pin down as a defined field of work. You don't see job listings for "Process Developer" and there are few, if any, official courses that you can take in Business Process Management.

The answer to this conundrum lies in the almost accidental way in which BPM has come about, and in the speed with which the technology marketing machine swings into action these days: usually before the technology is properly understood. Business Process Management is at the start of the "hype curve" and it will be some time before its key concepts become common currency among enterprise managers.

We will try to cut through this hype and the resultant barriers to adoption by presenting a practical step-by-step approach to the successful implementation of business process management. We won't spend a great deal of time on theory in this book; instead we will concentrate on building something of value to your business. Having said that, we won't simply throw together any old business process management system, we will advocate a project lifecycle approach, so that we implement business process management in the right way.

So what is Business Process Management anyway? Well, hopefully you are coming to this book with some idea of the answer to that question. However, Business Process Management, or BPM as we shall call it henceforth, means different things to different people. Each person's definition probably has some element that falls in the intersection of a Venn diagram of definitions, at the centre of which is the truth. One of the first things we have to do is to define what BPM means for us, so that we may set expectations about what will be achieved by reading and implementing the suggestions in this book.

This introductory chapter will lay the ground work for the rest of the book. In it, we shall cover:

- The business process management approach to developing software
- What a business process is and why you want to manage it
- Typical business scenarios ripe for BPM
- How this book will work:
    - The solution we'll build
    - Our suggested project lifecycle
    - Our example business scenario
    - Our example BPM suite

The BPM approach to software development

Business Process Management is the natural evolution and convergence of several powerful forces within the fields of software development methodology, enterprise application technology, and management theory. These underlying forces have all matured and converged at the right time for a productive fusion, which we know as business process management.

Evolution of software development methodologies

Traditional software development methodologies owe much to their engineering roots. The waterfall approach to software development was designed with the idea that building a piece of software is like building a bridge: the better your design and blueprint, the sturdier the end result. In reality, this approach falls very far short of perfection.

Developing enterprise application software is about delivering value to a business, and the business expresses that value as a set of business requirements. The problem with the waterfall approach, and the difference from bridge construction, is that unlike the laws of physics and the construction properties of metal and concrete, business requirements are subject to change. Businesses cannot afford to stay still: if they don't adapt to the marketplace then they will not survive. So business requirements are necessarily a shifting target.

Unfortunately, this is not the only problem with the traditional software development methodologies. There is also the problem of business requirements "dissonance". This is where the layers of end users, analysts, and developers create a chain of Chinese whispers, resulting in software that fails to resemble the original requirement. Each link in the chain puts its own interpretation on the requirement, until the end result is horribly different from what the business originally needed. This requirements dissonance can easily be visualized:

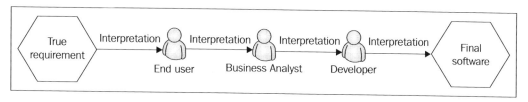

In recent years, the traditional waterfall approach to software development has been superseded by other, more adaptable methodologies. These methodologies attempt to break down the requirements dissonance by taking out the middle man as much as possible, and by creating prototypes early on, and then iterating them towards the final version. This allows for an iterative approach to software development, far removed from the "build a bridge" traditional approach:

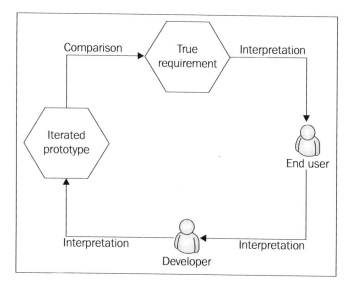

The most prominent of these newer development methodologies is **Agile**. On the right project, there is no doubt that Agile development can deliver valuable software more successfully, and more quickly, than the waterfall approach.

Nevertheless, Agile development and its ilk do have serious drawbacks and limitations. The first and most obvious limitation is that the Agile development methodology does away with the Business Analyst. This is an important drawback, because often the BA's interpretation of the requirements is more logical and more far-sighted than that of the end user who specifies the original requirement. This can mean that the developer can be led up blind alleys by an end user who doesn't have the necessary perspective.

There is also the problem that although we are removing some layers of interpretation, the layer of interpretation that we are leaving in place is the one that causes the most significant dissonance: the developer still has to interpret what the end user means.

This can mean that time is unnecessarily wasted on honing a prototype that starts off a long way from what the business needs. Indeed, some Agile developments have turned into one extremely long prototyping process, with an end result never being reached. This is an expensive way to develop software.

So what is the ideal, and where is Business Process Management in relation to this? For some idealists, the best situation would be one where the business users can build the software tools they need for themselves, without having to rely on developers or analysts. Unfortunately, although programming languages are becoming simpler all the time, we are still light years away from them being abstracted enough for an end user to build their own software. Software development is still hard.

Nevertheless, BPM does go some way towards this ideal, and given the right scenario, it can successfully deliver valuable software in extremely short time scales. In a similar fashion to Agile, BPM relies on cutting out the middle man as much as possible, only this time the emphasis is on a strong partnership between the end user and the BA working on iterations towards the final software:

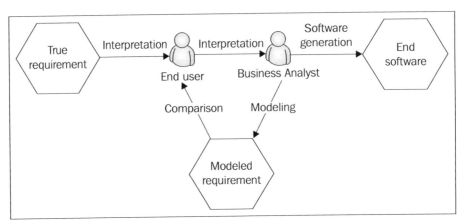

The reinstatement of the Business Analyst has several advantages:

- Firstly, the BA is skilled in the interpretation of requirements, and so their business process models are likely to be close to the original requirement.

- Secondly, a BA's models are far easier for an end user to understand than code or even prototype software, allowing for closer collaboration and faster development.

- Thirdly, the BA has the long term view and business skills to steer the end user's expression of their requirements in the most beneficial direction.

- Last, and by no means least, models can usually be produced much more quickly than working software. As the working software produced by a BPM system is initially generated from the BA's process model, this is an extraordinarily fast method of software development.

Don't be tempted to think that this means developers are no longer required, however. The reality of BPM development is that it makes the working relationship between end user, BA, and developer much more symbiotic and productive, but does not make any of those roles redundant. BPM is a partnership approach to software development; on one hand between the end user and the BA, and on the other between the BA and the developer. The skills of a developer are very much still required to take a BPM system all the way to implementation. Where a business process calls for the integration of other systems, that integration work will almost certainly involve an interface built by a developer. And while the software that is generated by the BPM suite is good, it does still require some development to make it properly fit for purpose.

It would be foolhardy to suggest that the BPM approach is the right one in every software development scenario, but it is a formidable new challenger to other development methodologies. Later on in this chapter, we'll consider some of the scenarios where a BPM approach is the most appropriate.

The emergence of key technologies

Workflow software has been around since the early 90s, if not before. These systems were most often used in document management scenarios, where a document (for example, an insurance claim form) was passed between different departments as work was done on it. This worked well because the workflow system only had to maintain a pointer to the document in order to pass it down the process chain. Where things got more difficult was when the workflow system met other, task-specific systems.

Most mature processes involve the coordination of several systems. For example, we might have one system to record our insurance claim, another to work out what payment is due on the claim, and yet another to make the payment to the end customer. Before the advent of internet technologies, and specifically XML, it would have been a mammoth and fearsomely complicated task to integrate and tie together these task-specific systems and their proprietary programming languages and data formats within the context of a process. This was quite often attempted, however, and the result was usually a development and maintenance nightmare. More code ended up being written to handle the interfaces than was actually needed to process the work.

Thankfully, XML emerged from the internet revolution as a simple way for systems to talk to each other without them having to know about each other's proprietary data formats. Many task-specific systems now implement XML web services, making the task of integrating them into a process relatively simple.

As a result, business process management can certainly be viewed as a repackaging of the workflow software that was available in the 90s, but the reality is that those old tools could never have delivered the same value as BPM, because the technology landscape has fundamentally changed in the interim.

Meanwhile—management theory

The third leg of the tripod that has raised BPM up to its prominent position is the focus on process in management theory since the 1980s.

What is a business process and why do we want to manage it?

What do we mean by "business process"? We typically mean a collection of business activities that takes one or more kinds of input and creates an output that is of value to the business. It is the focus by management theorists on the elements of this definition that has led us to BPM. This quotation from W. Edwards Deming, founder of the quality movement, is illuminating:

> *"If you can't describe what you are doing as a process, you don't know what you're doing."*

Any business process improvement project is an attempt to answer the fundamental question of "How do we organize our activities so that we can minimize inputs, maximize outputs, and maximize value?".

Business process improvement and re-engineering

There are several strands of management theory that are built around this fundamental question, and there are some striking examples where these theories have been effectively put into practice. Think of Jack Welch, who turned General Electric from a struggling manufacturing company to a highly profitable service-based company. Amongst other initiatives, this successful transformation can be attributed to radical business process re-engineering, and adoption of Six Sigma quality practices. Think too of Michael Dell, whose company of the same name changed the playing field of PC making and retail through a relentless focus on process improvement and ruthless process efficiency.

In business process re-engineering and improvement thinking, processes are viewed as organizational building blocks with as much (if not more) significance as functional areas and geographic territories. Business process re-engineering emerged in the 1980s with the idea that sometimes radical redesign and reorganization of these process building blocks was necessary to lower costs and increase the quality of service, and that IT was the key enabler for that radical change. The trouble with this radical approach is that it is too difficult to achieve in the real world. Mature organizations often simply cannot wipe the slate clean, and re-organize themselves without the instinctive memory of past processes and procedure creeping back in. Ultimately, business process re-engineering initiatives came to be viewed as nothing more than a cover up for downsizing efforts.

Business process improvement initiatives have been more successful, although they have been hampered by the lack of a comprehensive solution. Good-quality process design would be let down by sketchy IT support that couldn't be adapted. A business process would be designed around system constraints rather than systems doing exactly what the process required.

Nevertheless, many of the elements of business process improvement have proven to be useful and have not been discarded. Business process modeling has certainly increased businesses' ability to understand their operations and to make rational decisions about how best to organize their activities. Also, the definition and measurement of process metrics have given concrete, meaningful, and achievable targets for managers to work towards. The business is now more involved than ever before in the specification and delivery of IT programs.

From this convergence, BPM emerges

BPM is the final piece of the puzzle that allows business process initiatives to be fully successful. BPM espouses the incremental approach of business process improvement, but the IT delivery phase is supported by custom-designed tools that reduce the effect of requirements dissonance by allowing the delivery to be driven by the business.

In its simplest form, workflow software is generated from the process maps that are modeled by the Business Analyst. This workflow software is then the end user's "front end" to the process, and it controls the execution of the process in the live environment. Other software is then used to report on the operation of the process within the workflow software, allowing for dashboarding of key performance indicators. These dashboards can in turn be used to drive ongoing process improvement decisions.

Business process management isn't just one piece of software or one analysis technique: it is a suite of software, a framework of analysis techniques, and a defined project lifecycle. The Business Analyst, with their unique perspective on both business and technology, are in the happy position of having the right relationships and the right skill set to drive BPM initiatives in the enterprise.

Business process management: a definition

So now that we understand the background to BPM, it's about time we attempted a definition:

Business Process Management involves the graphical modeling of a business process, from which workflow software can be generated, which in turn will control the live operation of the process, interacting with both humans and other applications. Further software measures the execution of the process in the live environment in order to permit ongoing analysis and iterative improvements.

Key benefits of BPM

The buzzwords and hype that are currently circulating around BPM are presenting serious barriers to adoption. What's needed is a clear expression of the benefits of BPM. BPM delivers efficiency, control, and agility to the business that implements it in the right way. These three key areas of promised benefit can be further broken down as:

- Increases in productivity and effectiveness—a BPM system's task list makes sure that everyone is always working on the highest priority item, speeding the process along.

- Increased process compliance and governance—users of a BPM system have no choice but to follow the process that the system is built on.

- A more agile business that can change and adapt more quickly—because a BPM system is driven by a process model rather than by pure code, generally it is easier to effect system change, and therefore business change.

- Increased ability to scale best practices across a changing organization— once defined and built, a BPM system doesn't care if it has 10 or 100 users. Organizations that try to scale out a ten-man operation to a 100 person one often run into difficulties because the process becomes so difficult to control without software support.

- Improved communication, cooperation, coordination, handoffs—BPM systems are all about moving work from one team to another, reducing the need for teams to be skilled in communication and cooperation.

- Improved resource utilization—resources that aren't pulling their weight are very visible to management because everything that happens in the process can be reported on.

- Improved visibility of process pipeline—managers can easily report on everything that is in the course of being processed.

- More accurate operational forecasts—because managers have such good visibility of their process pipeline, they can more easily plan their operations.

- Greater process throughput—a well-oiled process running at maximum efficiency means that it will produce more of whatever the process is designed to produce.

- Higher quality output—because process compliance is assured, and because the process was designed in line with best practice, it stands to reason that the output of that process will be of high quality.

- Shorter process cycle times—with everybody who is involved in the process working at maximum efficiency, the total time it takes to run the process from start to finish will be reduced.

- Minimized cost of inputs—because the process that underpins the BPM system has been defined and because the BPM system leads the process actors through that process, there is a reduced need for high quality, high cost staff to ensure the process runs smoothly.

- Lower total process cost—the reduction in cycle time, the improvement in quality, and the minimized cost of inputs ensure that the total cost of running the process is reduced.

- Faster new hire ramp-up—all new hires need to do is follow what the BPM system tells them to do.

- More satisfied customers—the BPM system ensures customers get a higher quality good or service more quickly, and more consistently than they would otherwise.

Typical business scenarios ripe for BPM

Another barrier to adoption of BPM is a lack of understanding of the problems that BPM is designed to solve. Despite the persuasive benefits listed above, we must be clear from the beginning that BPM isn't the right solution in every circumstance. The following scenarios are good indicators of when BPM might be an appropriate solution:

- People don't comply with a defined process.
- The pipeline of work is unpredictable despite consistent customer demand.
- The actors in the process don't have meaningful targets for how much or how fast they need to process.
- Processes are carried out by disparate teams.
- Elements of the process have been outsourced.
- A business's reliance on a particular process has grown very quickly and best practice has not been adopted properly.
- Task-specific systems are not coordinated, causing breakdowns in the process chain.

Similarly, there are clearly situations where BPM is not appropriate:

- BPM is not appropriate for task-specific, procedural requirements: for example, calculating tax on an invoice.
- The business is so small that controlling the process would impose a disproportionate burden on its operation.

How this book works

This book is a full toolkit for someone who wants to implement BPM in the right way. This toolkit is particularly aimed at Business Analysts, although Project Managers, IT managers, developers, and even business people can expect to find useful tools and techniques in here. We will present the project framework, analysis techniques, and templates, BPM technology and example deliverables that you need to successfully bring a BPM solution into your organization.

The book itself is structured to reflect the project lifecycle that we advocate. Each chapter represents a phase in the project. Each chapter will talk through the theory involved in that phase, explain the techniques or the technology, and then show you how it is done with an example. Every chapter has specific deliverables that fit in with the respective project phase, and these deliverables will be worked through in the example. Templates for the deliverables and the working example can be found in the download for this book.

The solution we'll build

As we go through the project phases, we will put together our example BPM system. The process that we will manage will be a realistic scenario and the solution could be used in real life. The BPM system we'll build will be stand alone, without proper interfaces to other systems, although we will simulate an interface, so we show how it can be done. The solution could certainly be developed much further, and in the final chapter we'll see some pointers for how this could be done, but even without further development, the solution is fully working and useful. The most important thing is that we go through the project steps so that the solution we build is functional and effective.

Introducing our suggested project lifecycle

The book, and our suggested project lifecycle, is divided into six distinct phases:

- **Understand the target process** — to start off, we need to scope our target process, put together our project team, and then set about analyzing the process and building our first model for business sign off.

- **Develop the process** — now that we have our process model, we need to install our BPM suite and build our model within it.

- **Prototype the process workflow user interface** — once we've developed the process model in the BPM suite, we can generate a prototype user interface in order to run a proof of concept with our users.

- **Iterate the workflow prototype** — our proof of concept will turn up numerous process changes and user interface requirements that we need to capture, prioritize, and implement.

- **Pilot and implement the workflow** — we can now run a full-scale user acceptance test, and develop our key performance indicators that we'll track in the last phase. We can then put our process live.

- **Ongoing process improvement** — now that the process is in the live environment, we can monitor its execution and investigate opportunities for further improvement.

Introducing our example business scenario

Any business process can be modeled, but some processes are more suited to business process management than others. For our worked example, the process we will use will be drawn from the music recording industry: "Produce music products". As we'll see, this process fulfils many of the criteria we defined above for a business scenario that is apt for a BPM solution. It also gives us the opportunity to demonstrate all the capabilities of our BPM suite, so that you can adapt the solution for your own processes.

Introducing our example BPM suite

There are many BPM vendors in the marketplace at the moment, and many of them offer the full suite of tools that we are looking for. One option is to bring in a vendor straightaway, but given the barriers to adoption that we've discussed in this chapter, it is likely that a BPM project will have to prove that the concept is valid and the solution can achieve a return on investment before a vendor is engaged.

Fortunately, there are some open-source tools available to us that will, at least, allow us to prove the concept for minimal investment, and in fact are certainly good enough to provide a solution that is comparable to the best that the vendors have to offer. For our BPM suite we need a graphical process modeler, a workflow user interface generation tool, a workflow application server, and a process metric reporting tool. All of the following tools are free to download and use.

JBoss jBPM

The first element in our open-source BPM suite is the jBPM development environment provided by JBoss. This Integrated Development Environment, or IDE, is based on another open-source tool, Eclipse, which is widely used for Java development. The JBoss jBPM IDE gives us not only our graphical process modeler, but can also generate the workflow user interface for us. Here is a screenshot showing the user interface of the IDE:

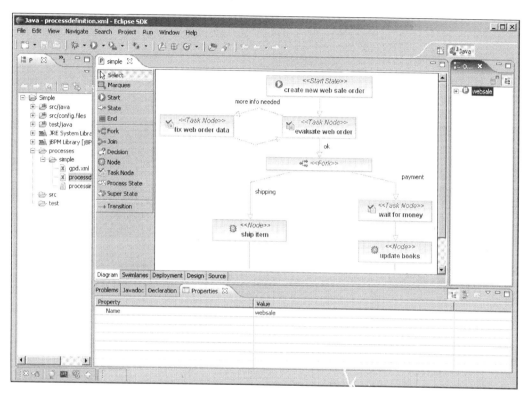

JBoss

The next element in our BPM suite is the JBoss Application Server, which is used to serve our workflow application to our end users. This workflow application is effectively a website, which the end users use to complete and record their process tasks. This is how it looks:

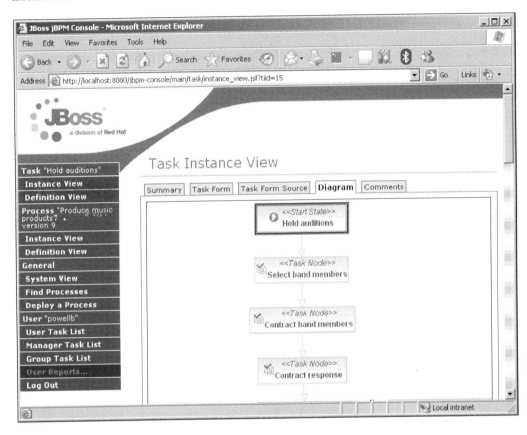

SeeWhy business intelligence platform

Finally, once we have our process in operation, we need to measure its execution. Our final tool in our BPM suite is therefore the **SeeWhy** Business Intelligence reporting toolset. SeeWhy is administered and configured over the Web using a browser-based console called the **Desktop**:

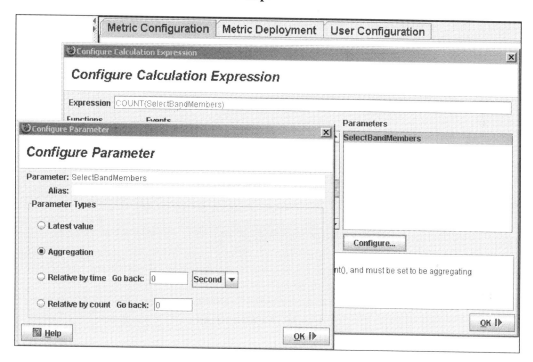

The second element of the SeeWhy platform is the **Navigator**, which is where our users will actually view the reports created by the platform. Here is a screenshot of the SeeWhy Navigator showing some business process metric reporting in action:

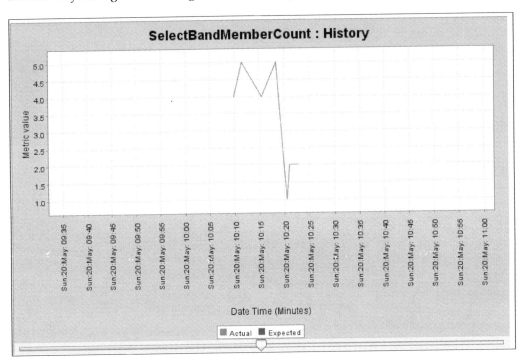

Summary

In this introductory chapter, we've set the scene for the rest of the book. We've discussed the background from which BPM has emerged, and we've seen how BPM fits into the wider scheme of enterprise application development. We've defined what BPM means for us, and we've looked at the business scenarios where BPM is the right solution. We have introduced our suggested BPM project lifecycle, and we've seen the tools that we'll put together as our open-source-based BPM suite.

Now, we need to make a start on our project, and have a look at our example business process.

2
Understanding the target process

The last chapter has given us a bit of background to business process management and it is now time for us to dive right in and get our project up and running. The project outline described in this book is intended to deliver a BPM system that is fully functional and usable in the live environment, although there will be many opportunities left for further development of the end product. The point of our project is to prove that the BPM concept can deliver value to our organization, so that management will agree to further investment and proper development of the system.

Given that our objective is of a limited nature, it makes sense for our project to deliver as quickly as possible. Nevertheless, in our haste we should not sacrifice proper project documentation and methodology, for without an audit trail, the concept will remain unproven. While this book isn't about project management methodology, we will at least describe how to initiate the project in a controlled manner, as it can be so vital to the successful outcome.

This chapter will also introduce our example business scenario, walking through the initiation phase of the project, where we'll define the success criteria and build our project team. We will then set about our initial investigation and analysis, until we build our first off-line model of the current situation. We will then apply some analysis techniques and produce a 'To Be' model of our target process, which our stakeholders can sign off as being a true reflection of their requirements.

By the end of this chapter, we will have considered the following deliverables that should be produced during this phase of the project:

- Project initiation document
- As Is:
  - Flowchart
  - Activity flow diagram
  - RACI matrix
  - Process metrics analysis
- To Be:
  - Activity flow diagram
  - RACI matrix
  - Implementation plan

This list of deliverables is loosely based on a combination of PRINCE project management methodology, along with business process re-engineering methodologies. Experience has shown that this is the right set of deliverables for a BPM project. Some of the deliverables may ring bells for you, some you may not have heard of; never fear! All will become clear.

Templates and worked examples for each of these deliverables can be found in the download for this chapter.

Setting up the project

It is very tempting at the outset of an exciting new project to just jump in straight away and start the analysis work, or even just start building. It is very worthwhile, however, to spend some time setting up the project properly first, so that everyone involved in the project understands:

- Exactly what we plan to do
- Why we are doing it
- How we plan to get there
- Who will do what
- When we are planning to do it

A cliché that is often bandied around on technology projects is the axiom "People, process, and technology". Typically, an IT project is good at addressing the process and technology bits, but all too often, the people element gets left behind as an afterthought for training and the nebulous area of "change management". The people element of the project needs to be considered at the very beginning, and concrete actions taken throughout to ensure everyone is buying into the project.

The very first thing that we can do to ensure we are taking our people with us, is set out our aims and plans in a project initiation document, and give everyone a chance to discuss these in a kick-off meeting. In this section, we will discuss the main subject headings in a project initiation document or "PID", which will in turn form the agenda for a kick-off meeting involving all the project stakeholders. Before this, however, let's introduce our example business scenario, which will serve as the source material for our example PID.

Introducing our example business scenario

We have been contacted by Mr. Sven Gali, CEO of Bland Records Inc., to try to help him turn around his struggling record label business. Bland Records has 200 employees and a turnover of $50 million, although in recent years profitability has declined sharply, until last years' profit and loss account showed a $1 million loss. This loss was made despite regular chart success and no change in production methods. Poor Mr. Gali is tearing his hair out in frustration.

Bland Records' speciality is in finding talentless, yet attractive youths, assembling them into bands of four or five, partnering the readymade band with a songwriter and some real musicians, who finish off the product with an addictive set of tunes. The end product is released on an unsuspecting public who promptly shoot the band to number one in the charts.

Bland Records is made up of four divisions: A&R, Production, Sales and Marketing, and Finance. The company is responsible for finding new artists, producing the albums, and then promoting them in the marketplace. Bland outsources the manufacturing of the CDs and relies on its relationships with its channel partners for warehousing and distribution to the end consumer.

Mr Gali has a tried and tested process that has never failed to achieve success in the charts. However, he has two main problems. Firstly, he has found that it is hard to predict his pipeline of new bands coming through, meaning that quite often one Bland Records band ends up competing with another in the charts, stopping both from achieving their full potential. Secondly, whereas five years ago Bland Records was the only record label in the industry with the foresight to manufacture bands in this way, now there are other competitors in the market, and these competitors have found ways to bring out new bands more quickly.

Indeed, Bland Records' main competitors, Sausage Factory and Packt Records, are able to get a new band into the charts within four months of holding initial auditions: unfortunately, it takes Bland Records six months. Mr. Gali is desperate to match the speed of execution of his competitors, without sacrificing quality of the end product.

Bland Records have retained our services to streamline their process, allow them to better coordinate their suppliers, and gain visibility of their pipeline.

Project initiation document

It is extremely wise to start a BPM project by creating a Project Initiation Document, and making sure the project sponsor signs it off. Having some level of project governance in place is beneficial not only for the health of the project, but also for the peace of mind of the client business. Project governance doesn't guarantee that a project will be well run, but it does at least show that some thought has gone into how the project will proceed.

The project initiation document defines all major aspects of the project and forms, the basis for its management, and the assessment of overall success. There are two primary uses for the document:

- To ensure that the project has a sound basis before there is any major commitment
- To act as a base document against which the project and its stakeholders can assess progress, change management issues, and ongoing viability questions

The very first action we must take is to identify our project objective. If we do not know what we are setting out to achieve right at the very start, then we stand absolutely no chance of delivering a successful project: how would we know we've been successful? We simply need to write down a brief description of the purpose of the project: a summary of what it aims to achieve and how. Clearly, the main objective of a BPM project is to implement a business process management system, although we would probably include some discussion of the wider business objective.

We must then identify the specific success criteria by which our project will be judged, and against which the project will eventually be signed off. Success criteria must be measurable, so that we can judge the success or failure of our project, as well as be able to tell when the project is complete. We should also include details of how these success criteria will be signed off, and by whom. The favorite acronym of project managers the world over is SMART, and our success criteria must certainly conform to this by being Specific, Measurable, Achievable, Realistic, and Time-bound.

We should also include a high-level project plan, so that we can set expectations for when the project will achieve its results. This plan should only include the major milestones, as a more detailed project plan should be prepared and tracked separately. Finally, we should specify how we will report on project progress: what, how often, and to whom. This wraps up the first half of our project initiation document. Let's take a look at how we might fill out these items of the PID for our example business scenario.

Example

Based on our initial discussions with Mr Gali, and the other executives of Bland Records, we are able to draft the following as a start to our project initiation document:

Project objective: streamline the process as much as possible, and then implement a business process management system allowing Bland Records to better coordinate their people and suppliers, and gain visibility of their pipeline.

Success criteria:

- The process time from first audition to album release is reduced from 6 months to 4.

- Pipeline can be forecasted and controlled, so that competing products from Bland Records are not released on the market at exactly the same time.

- The above success criteria will be assessed 6 months after implementation of the project, in order to allow the changes to take effect.

High level project plan:

Project phase	Duration	Start	End
Project initiation	5 days	18 December 2006	22 December 2006
Understand the process	9 days	25 December 2006	04 January 2007
Develop the process in the BPMS	11 days	05 January 2007	19 January 2007
Prototype workflow user interface	26 days	22 January 2007	26 February 2007
Iterate the prototype	26 days	27 February 2007	03 April 2007
Pilot the system	15 days	04 April 2007	24 April 2007
Implementation	20 days	25 April 2007	22 May 2007
Wrap up	5 days	23 May 2007	29 May 2007
Post project assessment	10 days	01 November 2007	14 November 2007

Scope the target process

The next heading of the project initiation document is "Scope". This can sometimes be challenging to fill in at the very start of a project, when you haven't actually yet done the analysis work that will allow you to answer the question. Still, it is possible to set rough boundaries, and indeed, it is normally worthwhile spending some time with the project sponsors and principal stakeholders to do a bit of background analysis to understand the organization. Generally, this up-front analysis work will pay dividends further down the line, as it will prevent the project from trying to tackle too much, or from choosing the wrong target altogether.

The first step is to decompose the organization into its processes. Typically, the business will see its organization as a grouping of functional silos, for example: Finance or Fulfilment. They probably won't immediately understand that what we are trying to achieve is an understanding of the business as a set of processes that cut across functional lines. Process is a way of thinking, as well as an analysis technique, and the BA will normally have to imbue some of this process methodology into the sponsor in order to be able to answer the scope question. One rule of thumb, which generally works well, is to describe the business as verb and noun pairs, along the lines of "Do something", for example: "Sell product". This helps to avoid thinking along purely functional lines.

For our purposes, we can define a business process as: "A collection of linked activities that consume inputs, add value, and produce an output of value to an internal or external customer". A diagram like the following can help impart the key definition of a business process to our project sponsors:

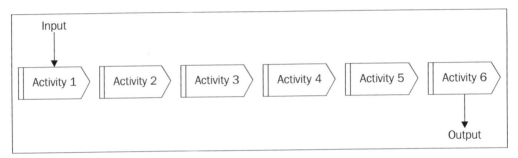

Generally, an organization can be represented as a process hierarchy, made up of 5 to 12 top-level business processes, each of which may have 3 to 12 sub-processes. Sometimes, those sub-processes can be further sub-divided into sub-sub-processes, but generally, these can be better described as "activities", which are the smallest unit of sub-process that we'd want to describe. For the purposes of answering our scope question, we would certainly not go beyond the sub-process level.

Through talking with our stakeholders and using our knowledge of organizations in general, we should try to build up a business process hierarchy diagram that looks something like this:

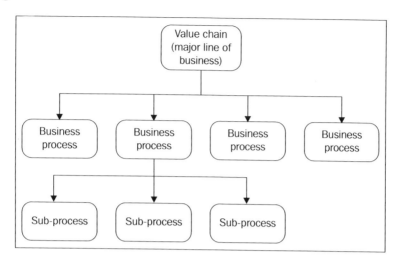

Once this is done, we need to specify which portions of the hierarchy we are going to target for our BPM implementation. In looking for the target process for our BPM implementation, we may actually end up selecting several processes, which when stuck end-to-end make up a core process string that we will seek to systematize. The processes must be consecutive in the end-to-end flow though, for otherwise, we will end up trying to build two completely separate BPM systems.

Typically, the most gains to be made from a BPM implementation are to be found by targeting the top level of the process hierarchy, as those processes will involve the most handoffs that can be smoothed and, as a superset, are likely to have the greatest impact in the organization. That is not to say that we should avoid the sub-process level, only that the benefits will typically be less significant. However, looking further down beyond the sub-process level would surely be a stratum of granularity too far.

In order to find our target process or processes, we need to investigate which have the most impact in this organization, which add the most value for the end customer, which are the most expensive to operate, and which have the most perceived problems. Once we've decided on our target, we should document this as the project scope in our PID: an amended process hierarchy diagram usually does this job very well. Let's see this as a worked example.

Example

From our discussions with Mr Gali and Bland's executive team, we have managed to work out that Bland has seven core processes:

1. Understand the market
2. Produce music products
3. Coordinate manufacture
4. Distribute music products
5. Manage finance
6. Manage operations
7. Manage legal issues

Mr Gali already told us that his main business problems are speed to market and control over the pipeline. We know that Bland Records don't have any problems with understanding their market because they consistently achieve chart success, and the last three processes wouldn't seem to impact on the business problems in question. So, given the nature of the business problems, it makes sense for us to focus in on the "Produce music products", "Coordinate manufacture", and "Distribute music products" processes. We therefore, concentrated our background analysis time with Mr. Gali and the other executives on these three processes, breaking them down to the sub-process level to amplify our understanding.

Having got this far, it became clear from our analysis discussions that the most problematic process is "Produce music products", so it was decided to make this the scope for our project. Perhaps future projects could build out from this starting point and address the "Coordinate manufacture" and "Distribute music products" processes, but it is sensible to keep scope manageable for this initial project. Having made this decision, we can pin down our project scope diagrammatically, and insert it straight into our PID:

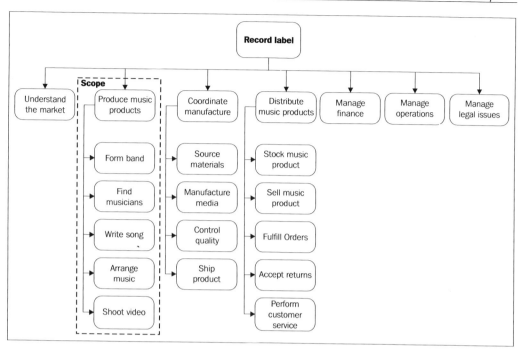

Put together the project team

Now that we have defined the scope that our BPM project is expected to address, we can easily identify the people to involve in our project team. We must specify this list of people in our PID, and invite them all to our kick-off meeting, so that everyone knows they will be expected to participate in the project.

Coming back to the old IT project cliché of "people, process, technology", we are extremely unlikely to succeed in getting people to buy into the project, if they are not involved from the very start. So, it really pays dividends to consider the make-up of the project team right at the very beginning, and to include everyone who might be impacted by the project in any way. If we don't do this, then no matter how great a BPM system we build, adoption of the new tool will be low because it will be perceived as being foisted on the user community.

The first members of our project team that we need to consider are our project sponsors.

Identify project sponsors

While the choice of every project team member is important, it cannot be emphasized enough how important it is to get the sponsor right. We need at least one and no more than three project sponsors, whose main responsibility it is to make resources available to the project: both human and financial. They must therefore, be of the correct level in the organization to be able to make such resourcing and budgetary decisions.

The sponsors will also set the strategic goals for the project and provide the ultimate sign-off that the project is complete. Any more than three sponsors will compromise decision making in the project and lead to unnecessary delays: the ideal is a single sponsor.

Project office

Now, we come to the people who will be accountable for actually delivering the project. We need to decide who will be the Project Manager, and who will be the Business Analyst. In practice, it may well be that these two roles are performed by the same person, but it is sometimes better to divide and conquer. Separating the roles can allow the Business Analyst to focus on the analysis work, instead of being distracted by budgeting and resourcing concerns. Generally, a specialist project manager won't have the analysis skills necessary for a BPM implementation.

The final member of the project office is the development resources that will be available to the project. There are choices to be made when filling this vacancy: for instance, do we outsource to a specialist development company, probably offshore, or do we leverage in-house resources, which would give us better long term support? Whichever choice we make, we are looking for a developer or developers who have J2EE knowledge, particularly around web technologies: it is quite unlikely we'll be able to find someone with JBoss JBPM knowledge because the product is quite niche. If we plan to integrate other systems then we need someone with interface experience, preferably web services.

Example

In our PID for Bland Records, we define our project office, including their roles and responsibilities.

Role	Responsibilities	Named individual
Project Sponsor	Responsible for the business case and for ensuring the project continues to deliver the business case throughout the project lifecycle.	Sven Gali

Role	Responsibilities	Named individual
Project Manager	All project management tasks within the project; resource management, planning, and delivery of a fit-for-purpose solution. - Financial control of the project. - Stakeholders' single point of contact. - Issue/risk management, resolution, and escalation	Peter Manager
Business Analyst	Responsible for performing the analysis activities, which will deliver the project.	Matthew Cumberlidge
Developer	Customizing the user interface. Interfacing to other systems.	Dave Loper

Identify process owners and subject matter experts

Next, we need to do some stakeholder analysis on our target processes to identify the owners of the processes, and subject matter experts who can tell us about the low-level detail of the current process.

In normal project management methodology, stakeholder analysis would be concerned with identifying not only those people who are involved in the process, but also those indirectly affected by it, or those who might be able influence it. For our purposes, however, we are seeking to determine all those functional roles, departments, or organizations that take part in or are directly affected by the operation of the process. All of these stakeholders will be process roles, and will eventually correspond to the swimlanes on our process maps.

The process owners and subject matter experts can be difficult to identify early on in the project, and often some of them will only emerge during the course of the analysis, but initial discussions with the project sponsors will usually turn up a list of the primary actor organizations in the process. These may include external organizations, as well as internal departments, and both should be involved in the project, if at all feasible: if not, then an internal resource close to the external organization should be identified to represent the external organization. The groups we identify at the start of the project will probably be subject to change as we go deeper into the analysis phases, but it is important that we do our best to be as accurate as we can at the start.

The primary actor organizations should be able to nominate a proposed process owner or owners from among themselves. We are looking for one to three people for process ownership. Process owners are empowered to decide on changes to the process. If more than three people are nominated as process owner, then we need to go one level up in the organization hierarchy, as we probably haven't got people who can make a multilateral decision. We will be looking to these people to help us with managing any organization change needed when we eventually implement our BPM system, so it is important that these people have the clout to make these organization changes happen, if they are needed.

Some further discussions about the operation of the process with the proposed process owners should enable us to build up a diagram of all the other organizations involved. We can then ask those organizations to nominate subject matter experts who can represent their interests and speak on their behalf in the project.

These subject matter experts, or SMEs, must have hands-on knowledge of the process. Generally, management-level people won't be able to talk to the level of detail we need, while at the lowest level the people might not have the cross-functional perspective required to understand their role in the process. Typically, we are looking for the sort of people who we might categorize as "super users".

The SMEs may well feel a level of suspicion about the project that will need to be dispelled. IT and process projects can sometimes be used as an excuse for headcount reduction, so it is important the SMEs recognize that the project is not designed to put them out of a job, but is in fact there to make their job easier. The SMEs must also realize that there is no "wrong answer": management won't be reading the outcomes of the workshops they are involved in, to ascertain whether or not they are sticking to current policies and procedures.

It is vital that the SME group we put together is truly representative. We must not only cover all the process roles, but we must also involve all geographic varieties of that process role. Process projects often fail because an assumption is made that a global process is performed in exactly the same way in every geographic location it is operated. It is extremely rare for there to be no geographic variances. Indeed, the alignment of global process operation is one of the principal benefits of a BPM system.

The SMEs have a very important role to play: not only will they provide the project with the vast majority of the process information that will form the basis of the BPM design; they will also act as advocates of the project within their user community, as well as eventually being key user acceptance testing resources. These responsibilities must be clear in the PID, and those identified should sign off the PID to say they accept those responsibilities. The selection and retention of good SMEs is the fulcrum around which a successful BPM project revolves.

Let's see how we will define our project team for our example business scenario.

Example

We decided to use a mind map to brainstorm those involved in our target business processes. Working with Mr Gali and his management team, we have been able to put together the following:

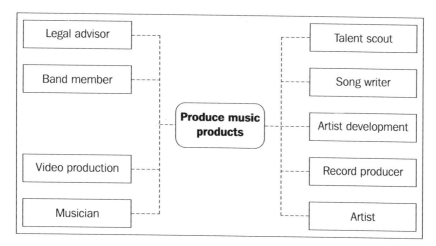

After discussions with each of the stakeholders, we have been able to define the process owner, and build up a list of subject matter experts. The head of Production was identified for sole ownership of the "Produce music products" process, as they had the organizational clout and reach to be able to make decisions for that process.

Each organization that was identified as a stakeholder nominated at least one SME to represent its interests. The named process owners and SMEs were listed in the Project Resources table of the PID, as follows:

Process	Role	Named individual(s)
Produce music products	Process Owner	Simone Cowell - Head of Production
	SMEs	Bob Jones — Talent scout
		Dave Jones — Songwriter
		Albert Jones — Record producer
		Kevin Jones — Legal advisor
		Marjorie Jones — Band member
		Susie Jones — Musician
		Graham Jones — Artist development
		Robert Jones — Video production
		Lindsay Jones — Artist

The PID also defined the responsibilities that these people had within the project:

- **Process owner**: once the process is defined, the process owner acts as sign-off authority for ongoing changes to the process. The process owners also manage any organization changes needed by the project implementation.
- **Subject matter experts:** they provide the project with detailed process information that will form the basis of the BPM design; they must act as advocates of the project within their user community, they will be key user acceptance testing resources.

Kick-off meeting

Now that we have written down who is going to be involved in the project, and what we expect them to do, we just need to get them to agree to it. The ideal way to get this sign-off is to hold a kick-off meeting in which the project initiation document is reviewed in detail, the named individuals agree in person to their responsibilities and to make themselves available, and the PID is placed under change control.

The kick-off meeting is critical for making sure that the team is aligned to the task: there's that "people" element again. It is also a great way to start building a bit of team spirit, and for getting everyone to realize that this project will require their active participation.

We can now get on with the interesting part of the project, analyzing the processes and building our models.

Analyze the process

We must now put our project team to work. The analysis phase of our project will roughly follow the five step process made famous by Dr Michael Hammer, that is to say:

- Identify and understand processes
- Share processes
- Measure and reward against process performance
- Improve processes where necessary
- Appoint a process owner

As you can see, we have already made a start on some of these activities, but the analysis phase will really deepen our understanding of the business processes. The key to success will be in communicating the "As Is" situation with crystal clarity to all the stakeholders, so that everyone has the same shared understanding. Only then will we be able to design the "To Be". The first step on this road is to very simply map out the sequence of activities.

Map the workflow

Mapping out the workflow as a flowchart model is a fantastic participatory exercise that works best in a workshop environment. The technique is low tech but extremely effective: we stick big sheets of brown paper up on the wall, and use Post-it notes to represent the activities in the flow.

Typically, the BA will steer the debate about which activity goes where in the workflow, and will ask questions to ensure all the steps are mapped, but it should be the SMEs themselves, who write down the activity names and stick the Post-it notes on the brown paper. This makes the exercise very involving, and the iterative nature of the task means that the end result is usually quite accurate.

Flowchart diagrams are made up of only two elements: activities and decision points. Activities should be mapped using one size and color of Post-it, and decision points with Post-its of a different color and size. The key is to define the sequence of activities, and to identify those points where the flow can go two ways, depending on the circumstances.

There are only a few simple rules to govern how the workflow should be mapped using the flowchart technique:

- Write the activity name on the Post-it note in as few words as possible.

- Write decision points as clear questions to which the answer is either yes or no.

- Don't get too hung up on exceptions first time through—go for the "happy path" first off, and make that go straight across (or down, depending on which way you are mapping).

- Make it clear that once a Post-it note has been put on the map, it isn't anchored there forever; they can be moved around to get the sequence right.

- The total workflow may take some time to achieve, so keep things moving.

- Don't start doing the "To Be": avoid the temptation to begin making workflow improvements while you are doing the exercise!

- Encourage everyone to join in—don't let anyone be quiet.

This exercise would normally be the first two or three hours of an all-day workshop. Once everyone is happy that the sequence is correct, they can probably break for lunch, and while they are eating their sandwiches, we as the BA can write up the flowchart in our process mapping tool. When they come back from lunch, we can present the written up version back to the group, make any small amendments that might be necessary, and ask for their agreement and sign-off.

Notation and Process Mapping Tools

The golden rule of process mapping is to always choose the simplest form of modeling that can communicate the required information.

Different analysts will have different views about which form of notation is best: from the very simple to the gothically complicated. We should always remember that our key objective, at this stage of the project, is that the model should enable communication between the BA and the business people, so that a shared understanding of the process is developed.

If the SMEs can't understand the model that is being presented to them, then they certainly won't be in a position to sign it off as being a true representation of their business. Hence, all we need are some form of activity boxes, decision diamonds, and later on, some swimlanes: anything else will just confuse.

Later on, when the communication target of our model shifts from the business to the developer, we may need to use some more complex notation that can convey a greater level of detail. The key is to choose the right notation at the right point in the project.

When it comes to process mapping tools, there is plenty of good software available. Microsoft Visio is a pretty good tool for mapping processes, and as it is widely available, we provide Visio process map templates in the download for this chapter. Another recent contender that you might want to consider is Gliffy (http://www.gliffy.com), which is effectively an online version of Visio.

Whichever tool you choose, make sure it can support the level of simplicity that we need at this stage. Certainly, don't be tempted to start modeling directly into JBoss JBPM: while it is a great toolset for building a BPM model, it is not yet a business-friendly process communication tool.

Example

On 3rd March 2007, a workshop was held in a meeting room at Bland Records headquarters, to which all the SMEs and process owners identified in the project initiation document were invited. The workshop was led by the project BA, and in the morning session they had a raucous yet productive session where they mapped the target processes as a flowchart. The following diagram is the written-up and signed-off flowchart that was produced during the session to represent the "Produce music products" process:

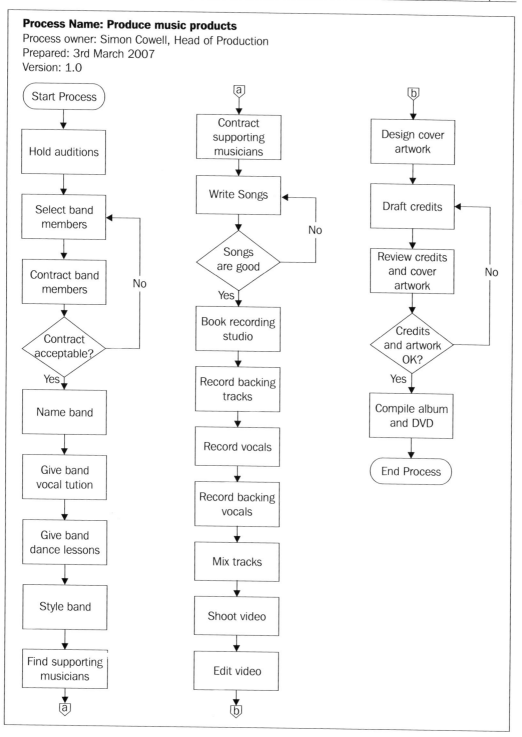

Process Name: Produce music products
Process owner: Simon Cowell, Head of Production
Prepared: 3rd March 2007
Version: 1.0

Start Process → Hold auditions → Select band members → Contract band members → Contract acceptable? — No → Select band members; Yes → Name band → Give band vocal tution → Give band dance lessons → Style band → Find supporting musicians → a

a → Contract supporting musicians → Write Songs → Songs are good — No → Write Songs; Yes → Book recording studio → Record backing tracks → Record vocals → Record backing vocals → Mix tracks → Shoot video → Edit video → b

b → Design cover artwork → Draft credits → Review credits and cover artwork → Credits and artwork OK? — No → Draft credits; Yes → Compile album and DVD → End Process

The flowchart was presented back to the workshop attendees during the day, and all present were able to sign off that the model was an accurate representation of their business process.

Identify roles and responsibilities

Now that we have the activities and the key decision points mapped out, we need to investigate the handoffs that occur between departments and organizations, as we go through the process. A great way to represent this visually is through the use of the Activity Flow diagram, which is more or less the same as a flowchart only with the addition of swimlanes to show who does what.

Activity flow diagram

Assuming that we have used the first half of our all-day workshop to map out the flowchart as above, the second half of the day can be put to use building the activity flow diagram. This will usually come together pretty quickly, as we have already done the hard work of defining the sequence of activities.

Working from the brown paper and Post-its flowchart we defined in the morning, we now need to identify which role is responsible for doing each activity. Note the use of the word "role", not "person" or "organization". Several people or numerous organizations could potentially fulfil the same role in the process, so it is the role that we need to define. Indeed, sometimes it will be tempting to assign one activity to multiple roles. This should be avoided for this modeling technique: a single activity should map to a single role. If this doesn't seem possible, then consider whether the activity should actually be split out into multiple activities.

The best way to practically assign the role to the activity is to write the role on the bottom of each Post-it note. Once we have gone all the way along the process flow doing this, we will have built up a master list of every role that is an actor in the process we are mapping. This master list now turns into our swimlanes.

Draw a swimlane on the brown paper in the same direction as the process flow for each of the roles you have identified. It is generally considered best practice to start with the role that is most external to the company at one end, for example "Customers", and to represent any "Systems" involved in the process, as their own swimlane at the other end of the spectrum.

Once we have all the swimlanes drawn out, we need to move the Post-it note from its current position into the appropriate swimlane, taking care to preserve the sequence of steps. At this point, it is probably helpful to draw arrows between the activities to make the sequence completely clear. Once complete, the team can break for coffee while the BA writes up the activity flow diagram in their process mapping tool of choice. Depending on how practised we are with these tools, this might take overnight; and it shouldn't be rushed for the sake of having it complete before the workshop ends. The important thing is to review the activity flow diagram, be it on the brown paper or the computer model, during the session when the SMEs come back from coffee to make sure it is accurate and no further amendments are required.

When the "As Is" process documentation is written up and complete, we should publish the formal documentation to a central location, and ask the SMEs to coordinate a review of the activity flow diagram within their wider user community to make sure any remaining kinks are ironed out, and to set a common language for future process discussions. One great way to publish these process maps is via an intranet: and indeed Visio can export maps in web page format to make this a bit easier.

Once all feedback has been taken into account, we need to ask for and make sure we receive written sign-off from every SME, and subsequently every Process Owner.

The great thing about doing this analysis work is that the model we have built is useful straightaway outside of the project: it can form the basis for training activities and can be very useful for providing context to new members of staff.

Example

The following activity flow diagram was created from the flowchart depicting the "Produce music products" process that was previously built during the workshop on 3rd March 2007. Going through this mapping exercise can often turn up more process actors than we previously knew about. This is quite normal, but we should take care to include the new people in our project team from now on.

Process Name: Produce music products
Process owner: Simon Cowell, Head of Production
Prepared: 3rd March 2007
Version: 1.0

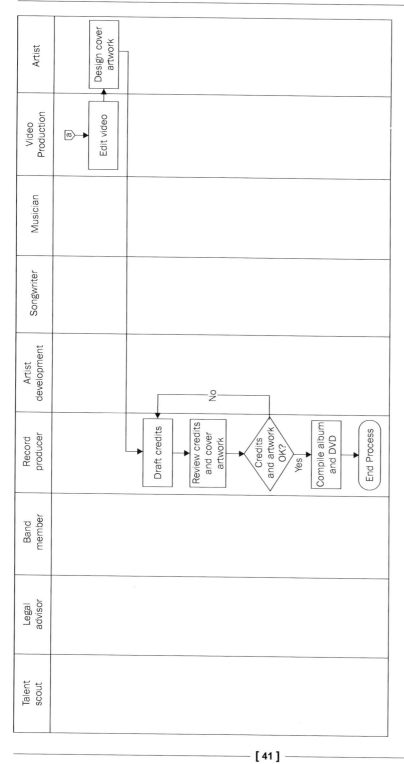

The finalized Visio diagram can be found in the download for this chapter. The process maps were published on Bland's intranet, and a week-long review was held within the user community led by the SMEs and process owners. At the end of the week, both the SMEs and process owners were able to sign off the process models as fit for purpose.

RACI matrix

Now that we have our signed off and published flowcharts and activity flow diagrams representing the "As Is" situation, we need to amplify our understanding of the process so that we can start moving towards the "To Be". One step along the road to the "To Be", one which can really come in useful later on when we build our BPM model, is to create an RACI matrix. This is another of those techniques designed to address the "people" element of the project, as it will eliminate ambiguities and ensure that everyone enters the debate about who does what.

RACI stands for Responsible, Accountable, Consulted, and Informed. The matrix has the activity steps we've identified down one axis, and the roles across the other axis. We then put either an "R", an "A", a "C", or an "I" into each cell of the resulting grid to define in detail the responsibilities and information requirements of each role at every step of the process. The end result is not only a great tool for training and bringing in new staff, but it will also help us understand both our task assignment rules and reporting requirements for our BPM system. Sometimes, the swimlane approach of activity flow diagrams can be too constrictive to properly express these subtle requirements, and the RACI matrix can help us get around this limitation and strengthen our understanding.

The rules for putting in the appropriate letters are as follows:

- Put accountability (A) and responsibility (R) at the level closest to the action or knowledge.
- There can only be one accountability (A) per activity.
- Roles can combine both accountability and responsibility for activities.
- Authority must accompany accountability.
- Minimize the number of consults (C) and informs (I).
- A for accountable means, "the buck stops here", and the role has ultimate yes/no authority.
- R for responsible means, "the person who actually does the activity". Responsibility for an activity can be shared, if necessary.
- C for consulted means, "kept in the loop", and implies two-way communication prior to the activity.

- I for informed means, "kept in the picture", and implies one-way communication after the activity.
- Don't map decision points on the RACI matrix, only activities.

It is absolutely imperative that all SMEs take part in the discussions to decide the assignment of responsibilities, and that everyone signs off: if not, then the agreement will not stick. The signed off RACI matrix becomes a kind of contract, and when combined with the process metrics we'll see later, it can form an informal or even a formal Service Level Agreement.

Example

All the stakeholders we identified in our PID and in our subsequent process discussions were brought together for a morning workshop at Bland Records' headquarters to hammer out an agreement on roles and responsibilities. The following RACI matrix was put together and signed off during this meeting, and clearly identifies who should do what at each stage of the "Produce music products" process:

Process step / Role	Hold auditions (1)	Select band members (2)	Contract band members (3)	Name band (4)	Organise vocal tuition (5)	Organise dance lessons (6)	Stylise band (7)	Find supporting musicians (8)	Contract supporting musicians (9)	Write songs (10)	Book recording studio (11)	Record backing vocals (12)	Record vocals (13)	Record backing vocals (14)	Mix tracks (15)	Shoot video (16)	Edit video (17)	Design cover artwork (18)	Draft credits (19)	Review credits and cover artwork (20)	Compile album and DVD (21)
Talent Scout	AR	AR	R					C													
Legal Advisor			AR						AR											R	
Band Member				I	I	I	I				I		R			R				R	
Record Producer			C	AR			C	AR	R	C	AR	AR	AR	AR	AR	R	C	R	AR	R	AR
Artist Development				C	AR	AR	AR			C								C		R	
Songwriter										AR										R	
Musician											I	R		R						R	
Video Production																AR	AR			R	R
Artist																	AR			R	

Key

R - Responsible	Actually completes the activity - responsibility can be shared. Degree of responsibility is determined by the "A".
A - Accountable	Has Yes/No authority - there can only be one "A" per activity
C - Consulted	Involved prior to decision or action - two-way communication
I - Informed	Needs to know of the decision or action - one-way communication.

Put metrics alongside the process

Now that we have the "who does what" part of a putative service level agreement, it only remains for us to put some benchmarks in place against which those people and organizations will be measured. The process metrics that we gather and estimate here are the beginnings of our Key Performance Indicators, which will form the basis of our reporting requirements for our BPM system later. As such, it is an invaluable stage of the process analysis phase and should not be skipped.

We are trying to achieve two things with this stage of our process analysis. Firstly, we are trying to analyze our process for value add, as this quite often turns up opportunities for quick-win process changes that we can implement in our "To Be". We are also trying to put a dollar cost against each of the activities we have mapped: firstly, so that we know how much we are saving by implementing our "To Be" quick win, but also for becoming the basis for our KPIs.

We start off with a simple spreadsheet that is similar to the one we used for our RACI matrix: process roles down one axis and the activities along the other. Then, for each activity in the process we evaluate:

- The value added; one of either
  - Real value added—something the end customer would be prepared to pay for
  - Business value added—something which is of value to the business, but not really to the customer, for example legal compliance, staff retention
  - Non value added—doesn't provide any benefit to either the customer or the business
- The touch time: the time that the process actor actually spends doing the activity.
- The cycle time: the time the process waits for the activity in question to be done, from the initial request to the eventual delivery. This is generally longer than the touch time as documents hang around in in-trays and so on.
- The unit cost of each activity. This should include loaded rate wage costs, equipment costs, and raw material costs to give a holistic view of the cost of each activity in the process.

Once we have worked out the above, we can calculate the ratio of touch time to cycle time, which indicates the amount of time a process devotes to doing useful work. Research conducted by companies espousing the Lean methodology has shown that in general, a well-run business should be looking for an overall ratio of between 3 and 10%. If your business has a ratio that is wildly different, it could be that your process is not as efficient as it could be.

We have to use stated assumptions about the per hour costs of different levels of staff, loaded with a provision for the cost of standard equipment, taxes, power, premises, pensions, and so on, in order to quantify how much it costs the business for each cycle of the process. We can then extend this analysis to calculate how much the business spends on this process per week, month, or year.

This is a truly wonderful piece of management information in and of itself, but when paired with the ability to plan process changes and calculate the resultant savings in cost per cycle, this is the forward-thinking manager's idea of nirvana. Of course, it will get even better for our managers. For now, we can only base these metrics on assumptions and estimates, but when we are capturing real-time data about the operation of the process in our BPM system, we will have accurate and definite numbers on which we can base future process decisions.

If necessary, we could use the metrics we've identified to draft service level agreements. This can be particularly useful where activities have been outsourced to third parties, although obtaining their agreement to the estimated metrics can be hard to negotiate, particularly if the real operation of the process is hard to measure. Our BPM system will help us with this when we have it implemented.

As all of this is difficult to understand without visualizing the result, let's see how we can put together process metrics for our example business scenario.

Example

In discussion with Mr Gali and our stakeholders, we built up the process metrics analysis table that follows. This analysis was enabled by the following assumptions and estimates:

- For the purposes of estimating cycle time, there are 24 hours in a day, 168 in a week, 672 in a month, and 8064 in a year.
- Open auditions are held 12 times per year and are held in a hired venue.
- It generally takes a week to contract all members of a band.
- Bland puts 12 bands together per year.
- Stylizing the band costs money in clothes, cars, and tattoos.
- The recording of the actual music happens very quickly: a matter of days.
- Shooting a video requires the hiring of a set and equipment.
- Hourly loaded wage rates are assumed to be:

  Talent Scout — $125   Legal Advisor — $187.50

  Band Member — $62.50   Record Producer — $187.50

  Artist Development — $125   Songwriter — $187.50

  Musician — $125   Video production — $187.50

  Artist — $125

Step #	Activity	Tal Scout	Legal Adv	Band Mmr	Record Prod	Artist Dev	Song wrtr	Mus'n	Video Prod	Art
1	Hold auditions	■								
2	Select band members	■								
3	Contract band members		■							
4	Name band				■					
5	Organize vocal tuition					■				
6	Organize dance lessons					■				
7	Stylize band					■				
8	Find supporting musicians									
9	Contract supporting musicians		■							
10	Write songs						■			
11	Book recording studio				■					
12	Record backing vocals							■		
13	Record vocals			■						
14	Record backing vocals									
15	Mix tracks				■					
16	Shoot video								■	
17	Edit video								■	
18	Design cover artwork									■
19	Draft credits				■					
20	Review credits and cover artwork				■					
21	Compile album and DVD				■					

Value	Touch time (hours)	Cycle time (hours)	Ratio touch : cycle	Loaded Rate ($/hour)	Wage cost/cycle ($)	Other cost/cycle ($)	Cost/cycle ($)	Number of cycles/	Cost per year ($)
Real	8	672		125	1000	2000	3000	12	36000
Real	0.5	168		125	62.5	0	62.5	12	750
Business	2	168		187.5	375	0	375	12	4500
Real	4	48		187.5	750	0	750	12	9000
Real	8	168		125	1000	0	1000	12	12000
Real	8	168		125	1000	0	1000	12	12000
Real	4	168		125	500	5000	5500	12	66000
Real	2	168		187.5	375	0	375	12	4500
Business	2	168		187.5	375	0	375	12	4500
Real	8	168		187.5	1500	0	1500	12	18000
Real	1	24		187.5	187.5	2000	2187.5	12	26250
Real	8	24		125	1000	0	1000	12	12000
Real	8	24		62.5	500	0	500	12	6000
Real	8	24		125	1000	0	1000	12	12000
Real	16	168		187.5	3000	0	3000	12	36000
Real	16	332		187.5	3000	50000	53000	12	636000
Real	8	332		187.5	1500	0	1500	12	18000
Real	8	332		125	1000	0	1000	12	12000
Real	2	168		187.5	375	0	375	12	4500
Business	2	168		187.5	375	0	375	12	4500
Real	16	332		187.5	3000	0	3000	12	36000
Total	139.5	3992	3.5%		21875	59000	80875	12	970500

As we can see, the process does show a healthy touch to cycle time ratio, and every step does seem to add some sort of value. This is good news for Bland, although it does mean that our opportunities for process improvement may be limited in the short term. Let's see.

Identify quick wins

In terms of a business process management project, a "quick win" (or "rapid implementation project" if you prefer!) is a process change that we can make to the "As Is" process definition, ready for implementation with our BPM system as the "To Be". This is not process re-engineering, which is a top-down, holistic, and cross-cutting exercise that takes months of analysis and impact assessment to achieve. Rather, it is about looking for simple process improvements that we can make without huge repercussions on the overall organization. We are particularly looking to cut down on handoffs, make activities happen in parallel, and ensure that each activity adds value in some way.

The following is a list of keywords that, if noticed in an activity name, should act as a red flag for a Business Analyst looking for a quick win. These keywords generally indicate that the activity is likely to not add much value to the overall process and it may be possible to eliminate it entirely:

- Checking
- Collating
- Preparing
- Accumulating
- Editing
- Checking
- Storing
- Retrieving
- Inspecting
- Copying
- Counting
- Searching
- Reviewing
- Revising
- Approving
- Filing
- Moving
- Rework

It should be noted that describing people's jobs as non-value-added can be rather emotive. People will tend to do what is asked of them, and so they can, through no fault of their own, work very hard at doing nothing of value to the customer or the business. Hence, the discussion about value added is generally best done with senior management rather than the SMEs.

Other red flags that we should look out for on our process map that might indicate possible areas of process improvement:

- Loops
- Handoffs
- Black holes
- Unused data stores
- Temporary data stores

- Overlapping processes
- Processes with lots and lots of steps
- Sequential steps that could be done in parallel
- Repetition

We need to use the visual and factual tools that we have produced through the course of this analysis phase to constantly ask the question "why". "Why are we doing this?", "Why are we doing it this way and not another?", "Why are we doing it and not an outsourcer?"; all these questions and more must be posed. It is worth bearing in mind that this constant criticism can be threatening to those being questioned, so it is important to prepare the audience for the barrage, and to employ a degree of tact where necessary.

Where an opportunity for process improvement is spotted, we must first evaluate the estimated cost savings of making the process improvement by using our process metrics as a benchmark. Eventually, once we have decided that it makes sense to change, we need to re-draw our activity flow diagrams and redraft our RACI matrix to reflect our process improvements. This set of documents becomes the "To Be" process, which the process owners will sign off and which will become the model and form the basis of our BPM implementation.

Example

There are not many opportunities that we can spot up-front in our "Produce music products" process, although there are a couple. Having looked at the sequence of activities, it seems clear that there are several activities that can quite happily run in parallel, and do not need to run consecutively. The following activities can be changed in this way:

- Write songs
- Design cover artwork
- Draft credits

According to our process metrics, changing these activities to run in parallel with other activities means that we can shave 668 hours off our cycle time. So, we have already enabled Bland Records to get their product to market 17% faster: Mr. Gali will be pleased.

The following page shows our updated activity flow diagram: our RACI matrix actually remains the same, because although the order of activities has changed, in this instance, the roles and responsibilities have not.

Process Name: Produce music products
Process owner: Simon Cowell, Head of Production
Prepared: 3rd March 2007
Version: 1.0

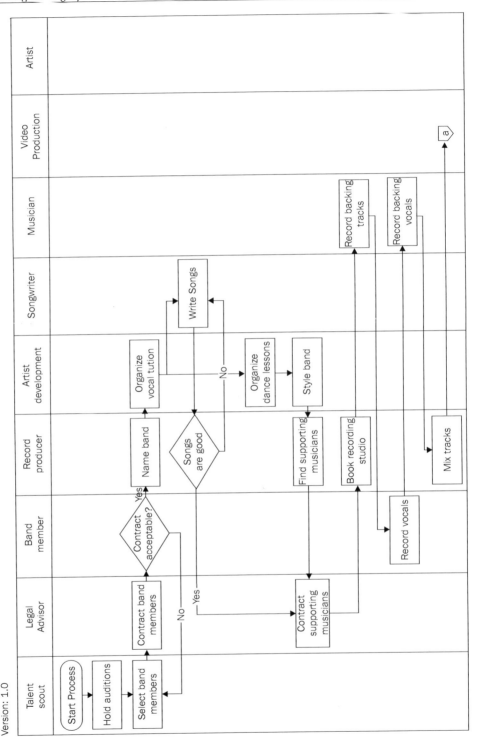

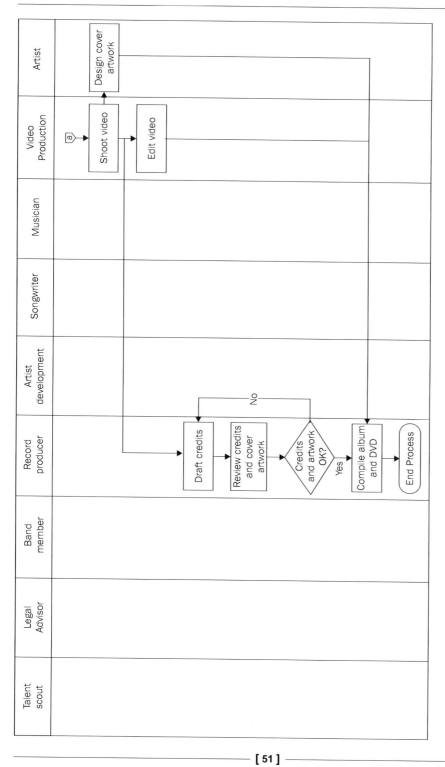

Sign off to be process

All that remains for this phase of the project is to publish the "To Be" activity flow diagram and RACI matrix to the full stakeholder audience, using our network of SMEs to communicate the planned changes. If the changes we are envisaging are numerous or will have a significant impact, then it is good practice to put in place a separate implementation plan. Generally, it would be sensible to plan this implementation to coincide with the implementation of our BPM system, as it is better to cause major upheaval once rather than twice.

Quite often, however, the quick wins are fairly small scale and there is no good reason to put off implementation, so a date should be fixed and the process change implemented as soon as possible.

With all this analysis behind us, we should now have an excellent understanding of the process and we're ready to start building!

Summary

This has been a whistle-stop tour of process analysis and improvement techniques. We have seen all the major tools in the process analyst's kit bag, with a view to creating a deep understanding of the process we are seeking to systematize in our BPMS.

There is much more to this than we can squeeze in one chapter, and there are plenty of sources for further information. For more detail and practical examples read the incomparable *Workflow Modeling: Tools for Process Improvement and Application Development* by Alec Sharp and Patrick McDermott (ISBN 978-1-58053-021-7), or *The Reengineering Revolution* by Michael Hammer (ISBN 978-0-88730-736-2).

In this chapter, we have considered the following deliverables of this phase of our BPM project, and we have seen worked examples of each where it has been appropriate:

- Project initiation document
- As Is:
  - Flowchart
  - Activity flow diagram
  - RACI matrix
  - Process metrics analysis
- To Be:
  - Activity flow diagram
  - RACI matrix
  - Implementation plan

3
Develop the process in JBoss jBPM

Introduction

This is where the hard work, but also the fun, really begins. We are going to get our hands dirty with JBoss jBPM and start building a process. Before we can do that, however, we need to get the toolset fully installed, and we also need to cover a few points of theory. Don't worry; we won't waste too much time on theoretical musings, as by far the best way to entrench understanding of a concept is to see it in action. The second half of the chapter will see us putting the theory into practice and using the tool to create our first process definition.

Compared to the previous chapter, the list of deliverables this time round is strikingly short. Nevertheless, as you will soon be able to tell as we go along, the length of the deliverables list is no indication of the required effort. By the end of this chapter, we will have delivered:

- Full working installation of the JBoss jBPM suite of tools
- A first iteration of the process definition for our target business process

The JBoss jBPM architecture

Before we begin the installation, if we see a visual representation of the software architecture, it will help us understand the platform we are going to put together. The following diagram shows how all the pieces fit together:

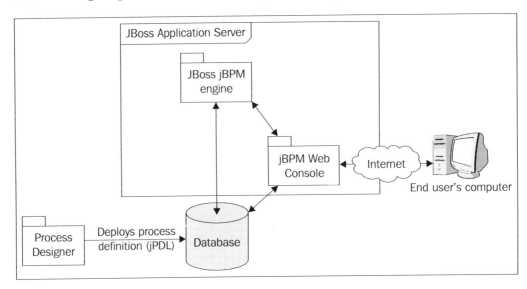

The processes are developed in the process designer, and the resultant process definition is deployed to the process database. The JBoss jBPM engine then interacts with this process definition to respond to requests from the jBPM web console as the end user uses the process application. The web console also stores the data it collects, in the process database.

Now that we've seen a quick overview of the software architecture, let's press on and get it all installed.

Installation

Installation is not particularly tricky, but there is quite a lot we need to do. We'll walk through it in detail, as it is easy to miss out a required step in the installation. The installation of Java products does generally involve a certain level of technical expertise. This installation tutorial has been designed to be as user friendly as possible, as it would be a shame if we got stuck at the first hurdle.

For the purposes of this installation tutorial, we will assume that your computer is running Windows XP Service Pack 2. You can undoubtedly install all the necessary pieces on other operating systems, but the instructions will probably vary from those presented here. If you find yourself in this situation, then you will find there are plenty of operating system-specific tutorials and instructions available on the Web in the JBoss documentation, readme files, and forums.

Here's what we need to do:

- Install Java
- Install the JBoss jBPM engine and the JBoss application server
- Install the process designer

All of these products are subject to ongoing development, with new product releases all the time. This tutorial will show you how to install what is available at the time of writing, but it is likely that newer versions will have come out by the time this book is published and you come to do an installation. Don't worry, it is unlikely the installation steps will change, just the release numbers of the products you are trying to install. Just use whatever is the latest available stable release and, if necessary, adapt the tutorial instructions to cope with any filename changes that have occurred.

Install Java

The first piece of the puzzle that we need to install is Java. Specifically, we need to install the latest version of what's called the "Java 2 Software Development Kit, Standard Edition". To get this go to the following location:

```
http://java.sun.com/javase/downloads/index.jsp
```

Unfortunately, Sun Microsystems, the organization that develops the Java language, are notoriously bad for re-organising their website and not forwarding on the old links. If you have trouble locating the Java Software Development Kit, search the site for "JDK"; you should be able to turn it up.

At the time of writing, the latest available version of the JDK on the above page is JDK 5.0 Update 9. In the **JDK 5.0 Update 9** section, click the **Download** link. If this exact version is no longer available on this page, just download the latest available version of the JDK, which usually appears at the top of the page, so you ignore the "With Java EE", "With NetBeans", and other bundled versions. After accepting the licence agreement, download the offline Windows version of the J2SE Development Kit.

Once the download is complete, run the executable file to start the installation. You can accept all the defaults given to you by the installation program. Once the installation is complete, we need to update a couple of settings on the computer so it can interact with Java.

Right-click on **My Computer** and select **Properties** from the context menu. On the **Advanced** tab, click the **Environment Variables** button. Then, in the **System Variables** box, double-click the **Path** variable. In the box that pops up, navigate to the end of the **Variable Value** line, add a semicolon to the end, then add the path to your JDK. This will be something like **C:\Program Files\Java\jdk1.5.0_09\bin**. Here is a screenshot of how it should look:

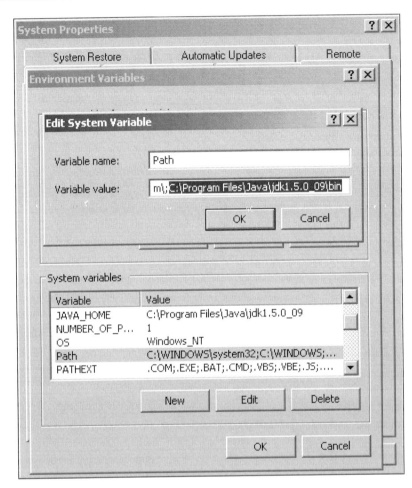

Now we need to do a similar operation and add a JAVA_HOME variable. Again in the **System Variables** box, click **New**. Give the new variable a name of JAVA_HOME, and a value of the path to your JDK installation: probably something like **C:\Program Files\Java\jdk1.5.0_09**. Note, in contrast with the Path variable above, this one should not include the **\bin** at the end. Excellent, that's Java installed, and the programs we are now going to install will be able to interact with the installation.

Install the JBoss jBPM engine and the JBoss application server

The JBoss jBPM engine is the set of code programs that run the business process management system. The engine is deployed in the JBoss application server. An application server can serve up any kind of application, from a website to an enterprise application. In our case, we are using it to serve jBPM and later on our web user interface.

Firstly, we need to download the file we need. To do this, go to: `http://sourceforge.net/projects/jbpm/` and click **Download jBPM**. In the **Latest file releases** section at the top of the page, you will see a row devoted to jBPM jPDL 3: this is the package that we need. Click **Download**. You will be presented with a list of files that are available for download. At the time of writing the latest available version is **jbpm-jpdl-3.2.GA** and that is what we will install. It makes sense for you to download and install the same version so that you can work along with the examples presented herein. There will be two files that you can download, one of which will be the "suite": this is the one we need so download that. You will end up with a ZIP file, which you should extract to a sensible location on your hard drive. I have decided to extract mine to `C:\MJC\Business Process Management\jBPM`. You should end up with a directory structure that looks something like the following:

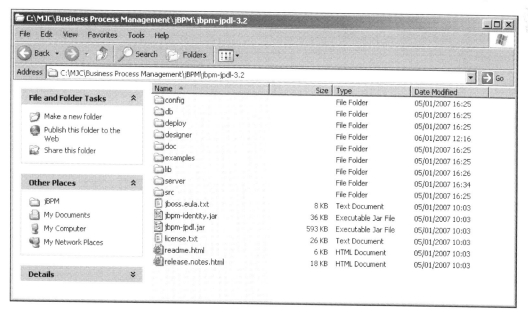

That should be all we need to do to install the jBPM engine and the application server. Let's make sure the installation is working correctly. Go into the **server** directory, and double-click the `start.bat` file. A command prompt will open up and the application server will be started. Don't worry about the stream of text that will be printed on the screen, just leave it running and start up your browser. Go to `http://localhost:8080/jbpm-console/` and you should get a screen displaying something like the following, which is the example workflow application that is bundled with jBPM:

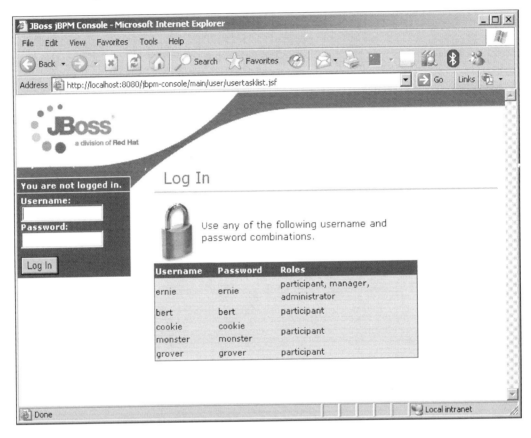

If you've got this screen, then congratulations! You now have a fully-functioning BPM system on your computer. If you haven't, then it could be that the version of JBoss jBPM that you have installed doesn't have the web user interface at the same location as I do in mine. Go to `http://localhost:8080/` and see what you have there. You should have something like the following, which is the default page served by the JBoss application server:

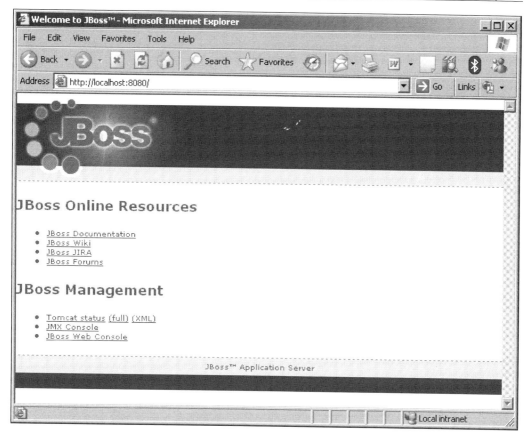

If you haven't even got this, then there is something seriously wrong with your installation, and you should go back and start again.

Install the JBoss jBPM designer

The JBoss jBPM designer is actually a plugin for the Eclipse integrated development environment (IDE). For those unfamiliar with the concept of an IDE, it really amounts to a tool that programmers use to develop software, rather like how we as Business Analysts use Visio or ARIS for developing our process maps.

An IDE normally has tools within it to help write and debug code. Eclipse is an open-source IDE that has gained a great deal of traction in recent times, particularly in the Java world, as it allows developers to write their own custom editors and debuggers that extend the base IDE. This is exactly what JBoss has done for the jBPM designer: written extra code for Eclipse to allow us to design and develop our processes in a visual environment. The jBPM designer plugin is part of the jBPM package we have already downloaded, but we need to download the Eclipse IDE separately.

The first thing to do is to get Eclipse. Go to `http://www.eclipse.org/downloads/` and download the 3.2.1 version of Eclipse. I downloaded the Eclipse SDK 3.2.1 Windows file, which comes as a ZIP file called `eclipse-SDK-3.2.1-win32.zip`. This is quite a large file (120 MB) so it might take some time to download. Once it has downloaded, copy the ZIP file to the `designer` directory of your jBPM installation. There is no need to unzip the file at this point.

We now need to build the JBoss jBPM plugin into Eclipse, so that the two work together. This is done with a little Java utility called Ant, which is used for building Java projects. Go to `http://ant.apache.org/bindownload.cgi` and download the latest release of the binary distribution of Ant. For me, this was version 1.7 and came as a ZIP file. Once this has downloaded, extract the ZIP file to `c:\Program Files\`. You will end up with a directory structure similar to the following:

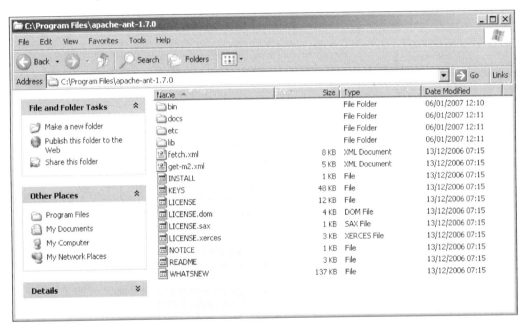

In order to use Ant, we need to tell our computer where to find it, in a similar way to how we told our computer where to find Java, earlier. Right-click on **My Computer**, select **Properties**, then go to the **Advanced** tab and click the **Environment Variables** button. In the lower dialog, scroll down until you find the `Path` variable. Highlight it and click **Edit**. A small dialog will pop up with the list of everything you currently have on your system path. Scroll to the end of the list, add a semi-colon on to the last entry if there isn't one already, then add in the path to the **bin** directory of your Ant installation, for example `C:\Program Files\apache-ant-1.7.0\bin`. You should have something like this:

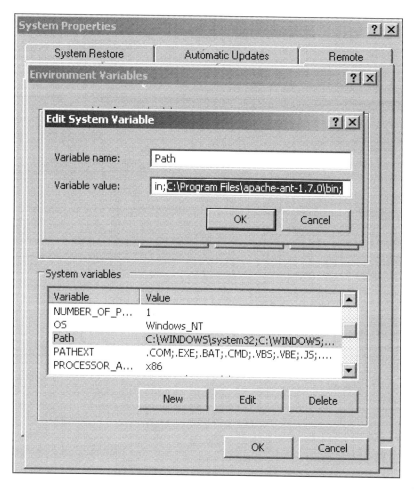

Click **OK** to save your entry. Now, in the same lower dialog, click the **New** button. In the window that pops up, add a new variable called ANT_HOME, and give it a value of the path to the top level of your Ant installation, for example C:\Program Files\ apache-ant-1.7.0\. You should have something like this:

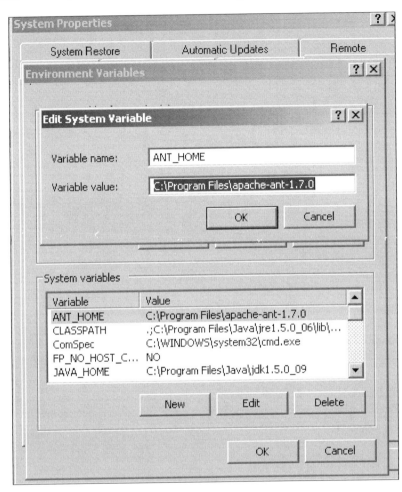

Now we have our build tool installed, we just need to specify some configuration for how Ant should go about building the jBPM designer plugin into Eclipse. To do this, open the build.properties file that can be found in the designer directory of our jBPM installation. The file will look something like this:

```
# the next property points to the eclipse zip file on your local
# machine.  the build script in this directory contains a target
# to get eclipse and put it in this directory.  in case you have it
# in another location, update the property below.
eclipse.file.name=eclipse-SDK-3.2.1-win32.zip

# Replace the eclipse.local.path with the uncomment version if you
want
# to supply eclipse in this directory.
# eclipse.local.path=.
eclipse.local.path=${user.home}/jbpm/repository/eclipse/sdk/3.2.1
eclipse.local.url=${eclipse.local.path}/${eclipse.file.name}

eclipse.remote.path=http://repository.jboss.com/eclipse/sdk/3.2.1
eclipse.remote.url=${eclipse.remote.path}/${eclipse.file.name}
```

All we need to do is tell Ant where to find the Eclipse ZIP file we downloaded and put in the same **designer** directory. To do this, simply change the code in the file as follows and then save the file:

```
# the next property points to the eclipse zip file on your local
# machine.  the build script in this directory contains a target
# to get eclipse and put it in this directory.  in case you have it
# in another location, update the property below.

eclipse.file.name=eclipse-SDK-3.2.1-win32.zip

# Replace the eclipse.local.path with the uncomment version if you
want
# to supply eclipse in this directory.
eclipse.local.path=.
#eclipse.local.path=${user.home}/jbpm/repository/eclipse/sdk/3.2.1
eclipse.local.url=${eclipse.local.path}/${eclipse.file.name}

# eclipse.remote.path=http://repository.jboss.com/eclipse/sdk/3.2.1
# eclipse.remote.url=${eclipse.remote.path}/${eclipse.file.name}
```

All we've done here is comment out the lines instructing the Ant tool to look in various places for the Eclipse ZIP file, and uncomment the line telling it to look in this directory. Once the file is saved, open up a command line (**Start | Run |** type in "**cmd**" then click **OK**). Use the **CD** command to navigate to the designer directory of you jBPM installation, then type in ant install. Assuming there are no errors, Ant will look at the build.xml file, see that it has to integrate the JBoss jBPM plugin into Eclipse and then go away and do the work for you.

The command prompt will confirm when it has finished, like this:

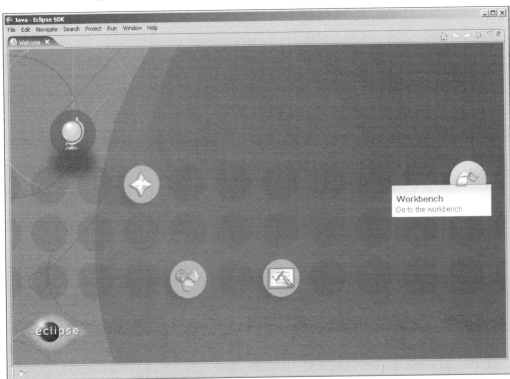

Excellent: we have now installed our JBoss jBPM designer. If you go into the `designer` directory, you will see a file called `designer.bat`. Double-click that file to start up the Designer. You should be welcomed to Eclipse with a screen something like the following:

Click the **Workbench** icon that appears on that screen. Go to **File | New | Other | JBoss jBPM | Process Project**. Give the project a name of **Simple**, and click **Next**. On the next screen, you need to tell Eclipse where to find the jBPM runtime. Give the runtime a name corresponding to the version of JBoss jBPM that you have installed, then browse to the top-level directory of your installation, for example `C:\MJC\ Business Process Management\jBPM\jbpm-jpdl-3.2.GA`. Click **Finish** to create the process project.

Once Eclipse has built the workspace, expand the project tree on the left and navigate to the **Simple | src\main\jpdl | simple** folder. Double-click the `processdefinition.xml` file that is contained in this folder. The visual representation of a very simple process will be shown in the main window of the Designer. This is created by the Designer when we create a new process project to give us a head start on developing our process:

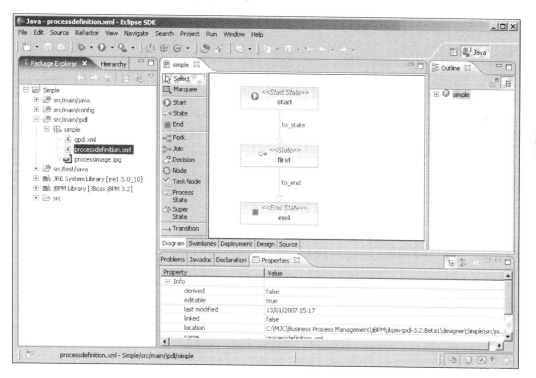

Wonderful, everything is working and our JBoss jBPM installation is complete.

Set up shortcuts

There is one simple thing we can do that, believe me, will make our life easier. Rather than having to remember where we installed jBPM, and then having to navigate there and find the right file every time we want to start the server or boot up the Designer, we should make some shortcuts. Navigate to the `server` directory of your JBoss jBPM installation, and find the `start.bat` file. Right-click on the file and select **Send To | Desktop (create shortcut)**. Go to your desktop and rename your new shortcut to something sensible like "Start JBoss server". Repeat the process for the `stop.bat` file to make a "Stop JBoss server" shortcut, and once again for the `designer.bat` file in the `designer` folder for a "jBPM Designer" shortcut. You can also make a shortcut to the end-user web console by right-clicking on the desktop and selecting **New | Shortcut**, then typing in `http://localhost:8080/jbpm-console/` for the location of the file to which the shortcut points, and calling the shortcut "jBPM web console".

Touring the designer's user interface

At this point, it is worthwhile having a look around the Designer's screen to get ourselves familiar with the tool. We'll see it all in action later of course, when we start developing our example process, but it is worth having a little introduction to the elements of the user interface, as they can be a little overwhelming at first.

Package explorer

The Package Explorer allows us to navigate through all the files that are associated with our process project, by expanding the packages within which they are held. For example, we have already seen the source files for the simple process with which jBPM pre-populated our process project. The majority of the other files in the Package Explorer are the Java elements of our process project: for the moment we can safely ignore these.

On the left of the screen you will see the Package Explorer:

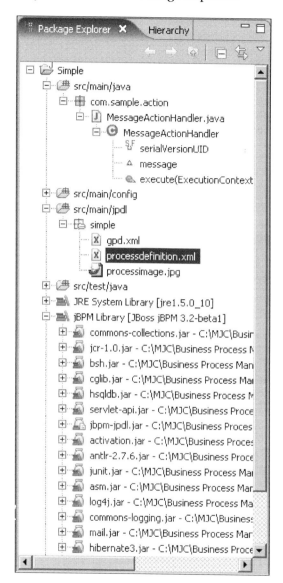

Editor area

In the center of the screen is the editor area, where the real work happens. This editor area is sub-divided into five main tabs: Diagram, Swimlanes, Deployment, Design, and Source.

Diagram

The Diagram view of the editor area is where we'll do the visual modeling of our process. We'll spend most of our time here, dragging elements from the menu on the left to build up the diagram in the middle:

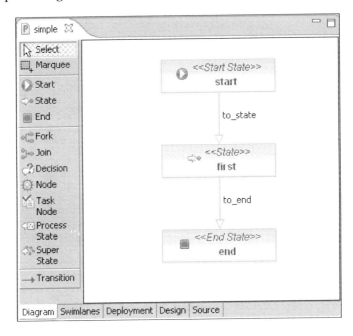

Swimlanes

We will use this view to define the roles of everyone involved in our process:

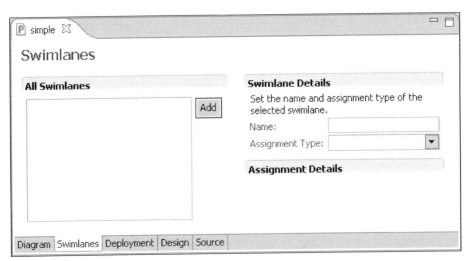

Deployment

The deployment tab is where we define our server configuration so that we can deploy our process to the live environment:

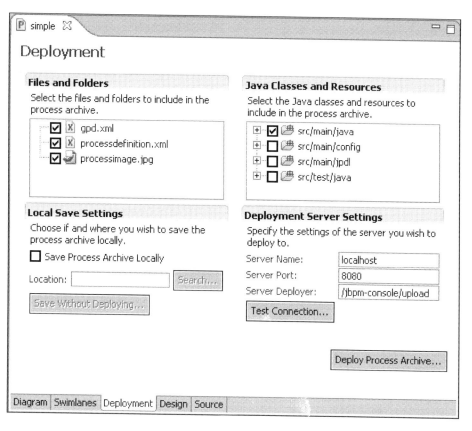

Design

The Design view allows us to browse underlying details of the elements of our process without the distraction of the visual map or the XML code:

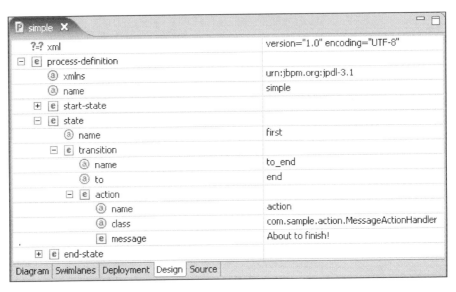

Source

Last but not least, we have the Source view, which shows us the XML code that is the process definition that underpins the process diagram and design. This process definition is what gets physically deployed to the server, and controls the process in the web console. This view is particularly useful for a developer, as they can use it to extend the process definition beyond what can be represented visually in the Diagram view by the Business Analyst:

```
simple  ✕                                                    □ □
<?xml version="1.0" encoding="UTF-8"?>

<process-definition
  xmlns="urn:jbpm.org:jpdl-3.1"
  name="simple">
  <start-state name="start">
    <task>
      <controller>
        <variable name="color" />
        <variable name="size" />
      </controller>
    </task>
    <transition name="to_state" to="first">
      <action name="action" class="com.sample.action.MessageActionHandler">
        <message>Going to the first state!</message>
      </action>
    </transition>
  </start-state>
  <state name="first">
    <transition name="to_end" to="end">
      <action name="action" class="com.sample.action.MessageActionHandler">
        <message>About to finish!</message>
      </action>
    </transition>
  </state>
  <end-state name="end"></end-state>
</process-definition>

Diagram | Swimlanes | Deployment | Design | Source
```

What is interesting about this view is that it is constantly kept in sync with the
graphical version of the process in the Diagram view. We can see this in action. For
example, if we drag a "node" from the left of the Diagram view onto the diagram,
and then switch back to the Source view, we can see that there is a new XML element
to represent this new node:

```
*simple  ✕                                                    □ □
      <transition name="to_state" to="first">
        <action name="action" class="com.sample.action.Message.
          <message>Going to the first state!</message>
        </action>
      </transition>
    </start-state>
    <state name="first">
      <transition name="to_end" to="end">
        <action name="action" class="com.sample.action.Message.
          <message>About to finish!</message>
        </action>
      </transition>
    </state>
    <end-state name="end"></end-state>
    <node name="node1"></node>
  </process-definition>

Diagram | Swimlanes | Deployment | Design | Source
```

As I haven't connected this node up to anything, the XML is quite bare at this point, but we'll see later how the XML is built up as we enrich the graphical model with detail.

Properties explorer

The Properties Explorer at the bottom of the screen allows us to see what properties have been defined for any element of our project that we highlight in the IDE. For example, if we click on the arrow labeled "to_state" in the Simple process in the Diagram view, we can see that there are three properties defined for this arrow (properly called a "transition" as we'll see later):

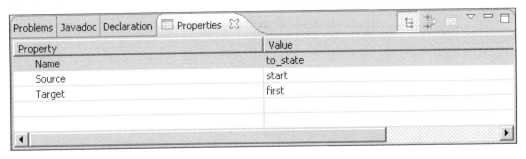

Outline view

The Outline view displays an outline of the file that is currently open in the editor area, and lists the main elements of the file's structure. The elements can be right-clicked to add various instructions and properties:

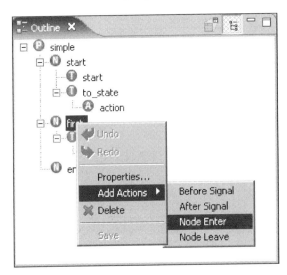

The Eclipse IDE is incredibly rich, and an entire book could be written about all the other parts of the user interface. However, we shouldn't get too bogged down in those details of Eclipse that aren't strictly relevant to the designing of processes, so for now, we'll move on and leave it to the reader to explore.

JBoss jBPM concepts

JBoss jBPM is built around the concept of waiting. That may sound strange given that software is usually about getting things done, but in this case there is a very good reason for waiting. Real-life business processes cut across an organization, involve numerous humans and multiple systems, and happen over a period of time. In regular software, the code that makes up the system is normally built to "do all these tasks as soon as possible". This wouldn't work for a business process, as the people who need to take part in the process won't always want or be able to "do their task now".

The software needs some way of waiting, until the process actor is ready to do their activity. Then once they have done their activity, the software needs to know what is the next activity in the chain and then wait for the next process actor to get round to doing their bit.

The orchestration of this sequence of "wait, work, wait, work" is handled by the JBoss jBPM engine. The jBPM engine looks up our process definition and works out which way it should direct us through the process. We know the "process definition" better as our graphical process map.

jBPM process definition language—jPDL

At this point, we have to get some core terminology out of the way. We won't linger too long over the definitions, as the best way to fix the terminology in the brain is to see it used in context, which we'll do as we start building our process. Nevertheless, we'll introduce the key terms and concepts here to get the ball rolling.

The visual process map that we have already seen in the Designer is an example of what the JBoss jBPM project calls "Graph Oriented Programming". Instead of programming our software in code, we are programming our software using a visual process map: referred to as a "directed graph". This directed graph is also defined in the XML representation of the process we saw in the Source view. The graph plus the XML is a notation set, which is properly called jPDL, the "jBPM Process Definition Language".

A process definition specified in jPDL is composed of "nodes", "transitions", and "actions", which together describe how an "instance" of the process should traverse the directed graph. During execution of the process, as the instance moves through the directed graph, it carries through a "token", which is a pointer to the node of the graph at which the instance is currently waiting. A "signal" tells the token which "transition" it should take from the node: signals specify which path to take through the process.

Let's break this down a little bit with some more detail.

Nodes

A node in jPDL is modeled visually as a box, and hence looks very similar to the activity box we are used to from our workflow and activity flow diagrams. The concept of "nodes" does subtly differ from that of activities, however.

In designing jPDL, the jBPM team have logically separated the idea of waiting for the result of an action from that of doing an action. They believe that the term "activity" blurs the line between these two ideas, which causes problems when trying to implement the logic behind a business process management system. For example, both "Seek approval" and "Record approval" would be modeled as activities on an activity flow diagram, but the former would be described as a "state" and the latter as an "action" in jPDL: the state element represents the concept of waiting for the action to happen, moving the graph to the next state.

"Node" is therefore synonymous with "state" in jPDL. "Actions" are bits of code that can be added by a developer to tell the business process management system to perform an action that needs to be done by the system: for example, recording the approval of a holiday request in a database. Actions aren't mapped visually, but are recorded in the XML view of the process definition. We'll cover actions a bit later.

There are different types of node, and they are used to accomplish different things. Let's quickly go through them so we know how they are used.

Tasks

A task node represents a task that is to be performed by humans. If we model a task node on our graph, it will result in a task being added to the task list of the person assigned to that task, when the process is executed. The process instance will wait for the person to complete that task and hand back the outcome of the task to the node.

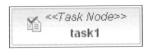

State

A state node simply tells the process instance to wait, and in contrast to a task node, it doesn't create a task in anybody's task list. A state node would normally be used to model the behavior of waiting for an external system to provide a response. This would typically be done in combination with an Action, which we'll talk about soon. The process instance will resume execution when a signal comes back from the external system.

Forks and joins

We can model concurrent paths of execution in jPDL using forks and joins. For example, the changes we made to our model to design our To Be process can be modeled using forks and joins to represent the parallel running of activities. We use a Fork to split the path of execution up, and then join it back together using a Join: the process instance will wait at the Join until the parallel tasks on both sides are completed. The instance can't move on until both chains of activities are finished. jBPM creates multiple child tokens related to the parent token for each path of execution.

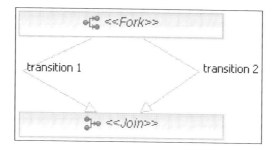

Decision

In modeling our process in jBPM, there are two distinct types of decision with which we need to concern ourselves. Firstly, there is the case where the process definition itself needs to make a decision, based on data at its disposal, and secondly, where a decision made by a human or an external system is an input to the process definition. Where the process definition itself will make the decision, we can use a decision node in the model.

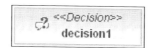

Where the outcome of the decision is simply input into the process definition at run time, we should use a state node with multiple exiting transitions representing the possible outcomes of the decision.

Node

A node of type "node" is a special type. It allows a developer to write a custom-defined node. Typically, this would be used when a developer needs to write some code to make the system perform an action, but the logic in that code is particularly relevant to the work of the Business Analyst, and they therefore want to see it represented on the graph. If it isn't relevant, then the preferred route would be for the developer to write the code as an Action, thus hiding the details from the visual graph.

Transitions

Transitions specify the route between nodes. Transitions can be named on the graph, if we need to make them distinct and choose between them during process execution, for example, if we are modeling two potential outcomes to a decision. If the transitions aren't differentiated like this, then the process instance will just take the first available transition.

Actions

Actions are aimed at developers. They allow a developer to add Java code to the model that will be executed, as events are triggered in the process execution, for example, entering or leaving a node. This means that we can include programming logic in our model without having to represent it visually. The action is modeled in the source of the process definition, but it doesn't show up on the graph. Typically, actions are going to be used when we need to do something in an automated way that doesn't strictly fall within the scope of the process definition, for example writing some data to a database.

Swimlanes

Swimlanes represent process roles, and they are used to assign tasks to specific people. This can either be one actor or a pooled group of actors, where one person from within the pool will pick up the task. Unlike our activity flow diagram, they aren't mapped visually in the process definition, but are added as technical details behind the visual map.

jBPM uses its own component to manage users, although in a real live environment, this can be replaced by a plug into the company's own directory of users, for example the Windows domain. Swimlanes can be modeled as users or groups, depending on which makes the most sense in the context of the process. Sometimes, tasks will always be assigned to an individual user, sometimes, they will be assigned to a group and anyone in that group can pick up the task.

Process variables

Process variables are the contextual data that a process instance builds up during its execution. Again, process variables are considered technical details and therefore aren't modeled in the visual version of the process definition. In our business process example scenario, we might have a variable called "bandName", which we would need to maintain as context for the process whenever we run it. If we can't provide our process actors with the band name when we ask them to do something, then chances are that they won't be able to do it.

Process state

Process state is used when we need to model sub-processes that sit within a higher-level process. This allows us to abstract our models and break down complex models into more manageable chunks. We may well do this at some point with our example business process as we have quite a large end-to-end workflow. This will help us keep our model clean.

Super state

Super states are a way of modeling a group of nodes. Typically, we would use this to group a set of nodes into a "phase" of the process. For example, we might specify a group of nodes within our process model as the "manufacturing" phase of the process. This will be a helpful categorization later, when we try to report on the operation of our process.

Building our example process

It is finally time to put these concepts into practice: let's start building our example process. We will go through building the "Produce music products" process in detail in this chapter: for now, we will simply concentrate on getting the process into the tool. We will worry about adding more interesting complexity at a later stage, once we have the bare bones sorted out. We are at the proof-of-concept stage after all, so there is little point in wasting time on nice to haves.

As a reminder of our To Be process, which we are going to build in the tool, let's have a look at the activity flow diagram that we built in the previous chapter:

Process Name: Produce music products
Process Owner: Simon Cowell, Head of Production
Prepared: 3rd March 2007
Version: 1.0

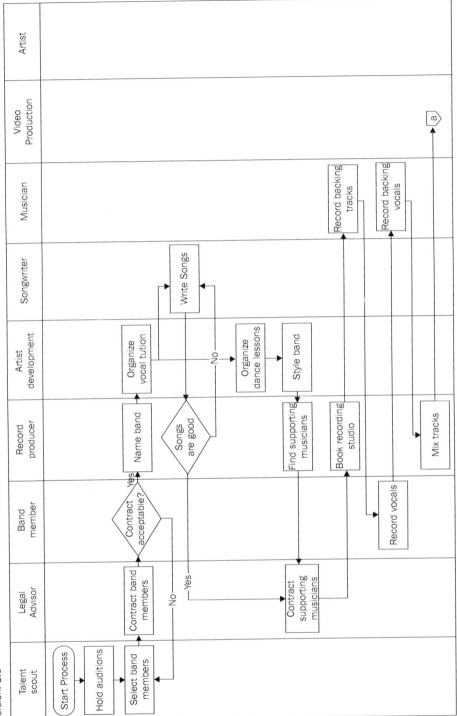

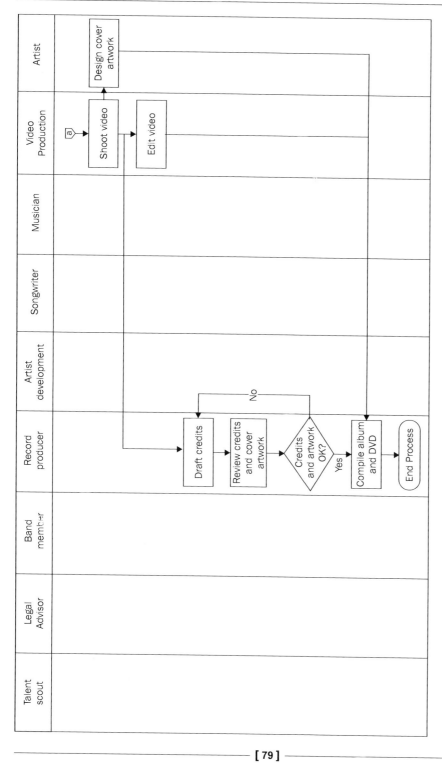

Open up the jBPM Designer, click **File | New project**, expand the **JBoss jBPM** node, and select **Process Project**. We'll call the project "Bland Records". On the final screen of the project creation wizard, pull down the drop-down box and select **JBoss jBPM 3.2** as the core jBPM location. Click **Finish**. In the Package Explorer, navigate to the **src/main/jpdl** folder, right-click on that folder and select **New | Other**, and then **Process Definition**. Call your new process definition "Produce music products" then click **Finish**. At this point, you can right-click on the "simple" process definition that the system autogenerated for you and delete it.

Add our swimlanes

The very first thing that we should do is add our swimlanes, so that we can assign tasks to people. Click the **Swimlanes** tab at the bottom of the main editor window. Click **Add** to put in an empty swimlane. Choose an Assignment Type of **Expression**, and then in the Assignment Details dialog add the expression group(talentScout). Once we have assigned tasks to this swimlane, this expression will mean that anyone who signs in and is recognized by the system as being in the group "Talent scout" will be able to complete the task. Once this is done, repeat the steps for each of the following, including the relevant assignment expression:

- Legal adviser — group(Legal adviser)
- Band member — group(Band member)
- Record producer — group(Record producer)
- Artist development — group(Artist development)
- Songwriter — group(Songwriter)
- Musician — group(Musician)
- Video production — group(Video production)
- Artist — group(Artist)

You will end up with the **Swimlanes** window looking like this:

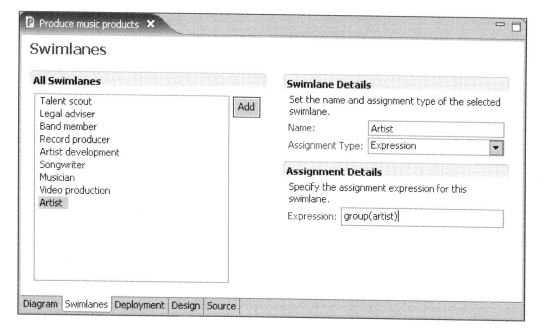

Adding our nodes

Coming back to our target process, the first few activities that we have defined are these:

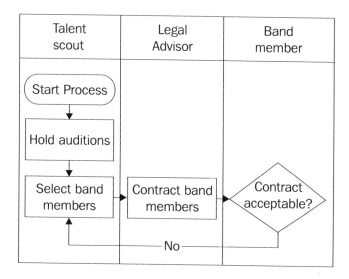

Obviously, we need to start off with a `Start` node, so in the **Diagrams** view, click `Start` node in the left-hand dialog, then click again in the center of the editor, towards the top to drop the `Start` node into the process definition:

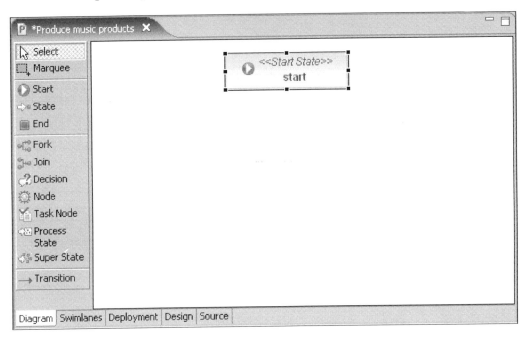

You can hold down the mouse button and drag the node into the exact position you require, if you need to. The first activity we need to model is "Hold auditions", and this is to be completed by the Talent Scout. Double-click the start node: this will open up the **Properties** dialog for the node. Give the node a name of "Hold auditions" and click **OK**.

Now that we have our first node in place, we need to associate it with a task. The task that we define here will correspond to what is actually seen by the end user in the web console they use to interact with the process. In the Outline view on the right-hand side, expand the tree view and right-click on the "Hold auditions" node. Click **Add Task** and then double-click the new task to bring up its **Properties** dialog. Give the new task a name of "Hold auditions":

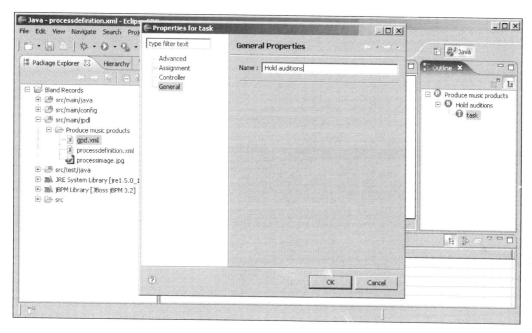

Now let's add a process variable to this task: this will correspond to a field on the task page in the web console, into which the end user will enter their data. We do this by adding our variables into the task controller: this element of jBPM maps the process variables that provide context for the process to the "task variables", which is what the end user will actually see on screen. This allows us to give the process variable a name that is easy to work with in code, but also give it a pseudonym that is more user friendly. The end user will see the text of the task variable name in the system at run time.

In this instance, we probably don't expect much more from them than to input the date and location of the audition. Click **Controller** in the left-hand menu of the **Properties** dialog, then click **Add**. Change the name of the process variable you've added to "audDate" by clicking in the Name column, then check the Read, Write, and Required fields for the process variable by clicking in the relevant columns. Finally, in the Mapped Name column give the new variable a task variable name of "Audition date":

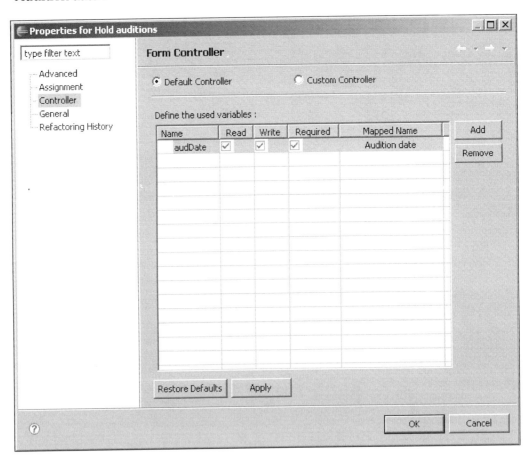

Repeat these steps to add another process variable called "audLocation", with a pseudonym of "Audition location". It generally takes quite a few iterations to get these process variables right, so don't worry if you find yourself going back, again and again, to the task definition to add more variables. Now, we need to assign this task to one of our swimlanes. Click the **Assignment** menu item in the left-hand pane, then choose an assignment type of **Swimlane**. Choose the "Talent scout" swimlane to assign them to this task, and then click **OK** to finish defining the task node. Congratulations, you've defined your first task in the process!

You will notice that we use a rather strange naming convention for our process variables, mixing up letter case and running the words together. We are employing the Java naming convention for our variables, as this will make it easy for our developer to work with them when the time comes. We simply start the first word with a lower case letter, then remove spaces between the other words, with each subsequent word starting with a capital letter. So for example, "My Hair Color" becomes "myHairColor".

The next activity we need to define is the "Select band members" activity. As this is a task that is to be performed by a human, we will model this in jPDL as a task node. Click **Task Node** in the left-hand dialog, and then click again underneath the start node to drop the task node on the process definition. As before, double-click the new node to rename it as "Select band members". If the text is too long for the task node box, you can click the box then drag the handles to resize the box to fit the text. As we did with the previous node, add a task of "Select band members", and assign it to the "Talent Scout" swimlane. We are going to use our process variables to hold the names of our band members. Bland records have a policy of creating bands of minimum three and maximum six people. To reflect this business rule, we are going to add six process variables: "bm1", "bm2", "bm3", "bm4", "bm5", and "bm6", each with a pseudonym of "Band member *x*", where "*x*" is to be replaced with the relevant number. We will make all of these process variables Read and Write, but only "bm1", "bm2", and "bm3" will be required fields. The user can then leave 4, 5, and 6 blank if they don't need them.

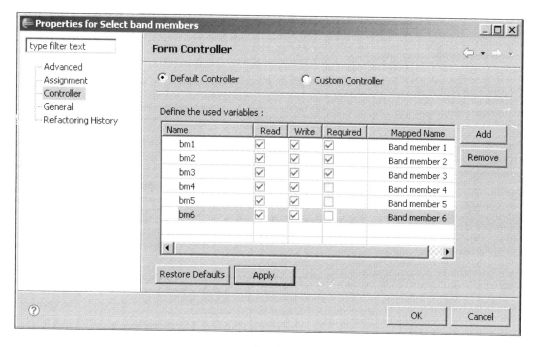

Now, we need to add the transition to the process graph that will take us from the "Hold auditions" node to the "Select band members" node. Click **Transition** in the left-hand dialog, then click the "Hold auditions" node followed by the "Select band members" node. The transition arrow will be added to the process definition:

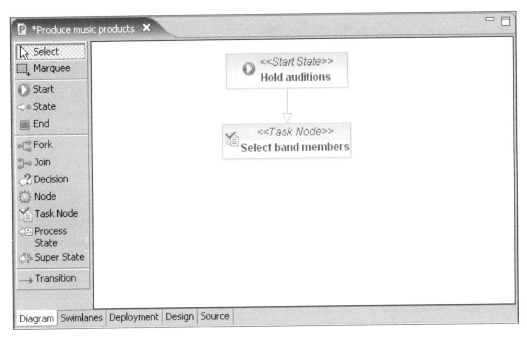

We then add another task node and task called "Contract band members", assigning it to the Legal adviser swimlane. We'll give it Read and Write process variables of "bm1ContractSent" to "bm6ContractSent" (with pseudonyms of "Band member *x* contract sent?"), with only 1, 2 and 3 being required in order to be consistent with the previous node.

Now we come to our first decision on the activity flow diagram, "Contract acceptable?". It is the band members themselves who are making this decision, although it is important for us to note from a BPM perspective that they may not actually be the ones who input the outcome of their decision into the system. In fact, from a design point of view, it would probably make most sense for our trusty legal adviser to gather the band members' responses to the contract and input the outcome into the system. This is quite a common scenario when developing a BPM system: quite often you don't want to give every possible process actor access to your system, rather you maintain a core group of internal users, who sometimes record the outcome of tasks done by other process actors outside of the system.

The behavior that we therefore want to model here is for the legal adviser to be able to record whether or not all our band members are happy with the contract. If they are, then great, the process can proceed. If not, then we need to select some more band members and try again. So we are going to model this as three nodes: one task node where the legal adviser will input the decision of each of the band members, a second task node where the Legal Adviser will check to see if any of these decisions are a "No", in which case we'll go to a third node where a new band member can be input and contracted. When we finally have a "Yes" for all of our band members, we'll continue on to the next node. To do this, we define the following:

Node name	Node type	Task name	Swimlane	Process variables
Contract response	Task node	Contract response	Legal adviser	bm1Agreed — R/W — Band member 1 agreed?
				bm2Agreed — R/W — Band member 2 agreed?
				bm3Agreed — R/W — Band member 3 agreed?
				bm4Agreed — R/W — Band member 4 agreed?
				bm5Agreed — R/W — Band member 5 agreed?
				bm6Agreed — R/W — Band member 6 agreed?
All contracts agreed?	Task node	All contracts agreed?	Legal adviser	bm1Agreed — R — Band member 1 agreed?
				bm2Agreed — R — Band member 2 agreed?
				bm3Agreed — R — Band member 3 agreed?
				bm4Agreed — R — Band member 4 agreed?
				bm5Agreed — R — Band member 5 agreed?
				bm6Agreed — R — Band member 6 agreed?

Node name	Node type	Task name	Swimlane	Process variables
Contract new member	Task node	Contract new member	Legal adviser	bm1 — R/W/Req — Band member 1
				bm2 — R/W/Req — Band member 2
				bm3 — R/W/Req — Band member 3
				bm4 — R/W — Band member 4
				bm5 — R/W — Band member 5
				bm6 — R/W — Band member 6
				bm1Agreed — R/W — Band member 1 agreed?
				bm2Agreed — R/W — Band member 2 agreed?
				bm3Agreed — R/W — Band member 3 agreed?
				bm4Agreed — R/W — Band member 4 agreed?
				bm5Agreed — R/W — Band member 5 agreed?
				bm6Agreed — R/W — Band member 6 agreed?

Note that we make all the "bmx" process variables Read and Write, but in this instance we don't make any of them required, as we don't know which of the band members will not agree to the contract and hence which we'll need to replace. Note also that we make the bmxAgreed variables in the "All contracts agreed?" node read-only, as the Legal adviser is merely evaluating the data they have previously input in this node.

We also need a transition going out sideways from "All contracts agreed?" to "Contract new member", and this needs to be named "No", with a further unnamed transition coming back from "Contract new member" into "All contracts agreed?". Finally, we have another transition coming out of "All contracts agreed?", and named "Yes" and going into the next node in the process, which we'll leave blank for now. You name a transition by clicking on it and then typing the name into the appropriate box in the Properties window at the bottom of the screen.

Note that you can drag a transition arrow out to an angle to make it easier to differentiate between incoming and outgoing transitions. When you've finished doing all this your graph should look something like this:

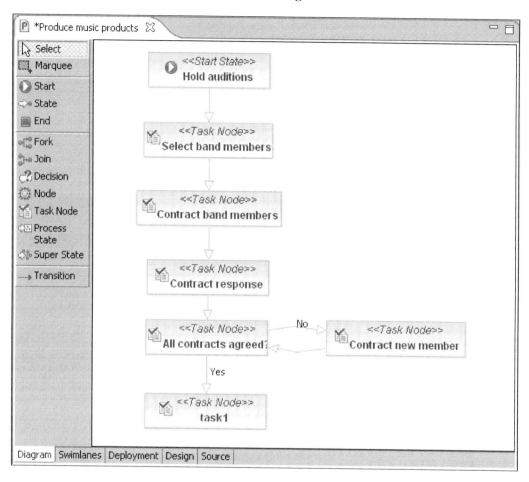

That's it, we've finished modeling the decision. We have actually opted for quite a simple way of implementing this decision point. jPDL does allow us to implement decisions in more complex ways. For example, we could have implemented the "All contracts agreed?" node as a decision node, then used some scripting to automatically evaluate whether any of the bmxAgreed variables was set to "No". Both methods are equally valid, but for the sake of simplicity we will try to use our human process actors as much as possible, at least for the first iteration of our process definition. Later on, when we are more comfortable with the system and with working with process variables, we may re-work some of these decisions as automated system-determined decision nodes.

As you can see, defining a process for implementation in a BPM often involves breaking down an activity into several constituent parts to produce a logical flow that will make sense in the resulting user interface. It is an important skill for the process designer to be able to visualize how their model will work when it is deployed as the final user interface. Don't worry too much though, it is practically impossible to get this right the first time, and almost always some iteration will be required once the user interface is deployed, and you can see how your well thought out model actually turned out.

At this point, it is worthwhile taking a brief look at the XML we are building up in the Source view:

```xml
<?xml version="1.0" encoding="UTF-8"?>

<process-definition
    xmlns="urn:jbpm.org:jpdl-3.2"  name="Produce music products">

    <swimlane name="Talent scout">
        <assignment expression="group(talentScout)"></assignment>
    </swimlane>

    ...we've missed some out here for brevity...

    <start-state name="Hold auditions">

        <task name="Hold auditions" swimlane="Talent scout">
            <controller>
                <variable name="audDate" access="read,write,required"
mapped-name="Audition date"></variable>
                <variable name="audLocation" access="read,write,required"
mapped-name="Audition location"></variable>
            </controller>
        </task>
        <transition name="" to="Select band members"></transition>
    </start-state>
    <task-node name="Select band members">
        <task name="Select band members" swimlane="Talent scout">
            <controller>
                <variable name="bm1" access="read,write,required" mapped-
name="Band member 1"></variable>
                <variable name="bm2" access="read,write,required" mapped-
name="Band member 2"></variable>
                <variable name="bm3" access="read,write,required" mapped-
name="Band member 3"></variable>
                <variable name="bm4" mapped-name="Band member 4"></
variable>
                <variable name="bm5" mapped-name="Band member 5"></
variable>
```

```
            <variable name="bm6" mapped-name="Band member 6"></
variable>
        </controller>
      </task>
      <transition name="" to="Contract band members"></transition>
    </task-node>

... and we've removed some here too ...

    <task-node name="All contracts agreed?">
      <task name="All contracts agreed?" swimlane="Legal adviser">
        <controller>
          <variable name="bm1Agreed" access="read" mapped-name="Band
member 1 agreed?"></variable>
          <variable name="bm2Agreed" access="read" mapped-name="Band
member 2 agreed?"></variable>
          <variable name="bm3Agreed" access="read" mapped-name="Band
member 3 agreed?"></variable>
          <variable name="bm4Agreed" access="read" mapped-name="Band
member 4 agreed?"></variable>
          <variable name="bm5Agreed" access="read" mapped-name="Band
member 5 agreed?"></variable>
          <variable name="bm6Agreed" access="read" mapped-name="Band
member 6 agreed?"></variable>
        </controller>
      </task>
      <transition name="No" to="Contract new member"></transition>
      <transition name="Yes" to="task1"></transition>
    </task-node>

... and here ...

      <transition name="" to="All contracts agreed?"></transition>
    </task-node>
    <task-node name="task1">
    </task-node>
</process-definition>
```

You can clearly see how the elements we have been mapping visually and in the Properties dialog boxes are being translated to the XML source code. We don't need to worry about this at all right now, but it is worthwhile starting to become familiar with the syntax as we will be hooking into this code in later chapters.

The next two steps in our process, "Name band" and "Organize vocal tuition" are straightforward, and as we've already seen how to build regular task nodes we won't linger over the details. You can see how we've built them for yourself in the process definition included in the download for this chapter. To install the process definition from the download:

1. Highlight the `src/main/jpdl` folder in the Package explorer.

2. Click **File | Import**.

3. In the resultant dialog, expand **General** and choose **File System**, then **Next**.

4. Browse to the directory where you have extracted the download for the chapter. Highlight the **Produce music products** folder.

5. Check the boxes next to the all of the files that the Designer finds.

6. Click **Finish**.

After "Organize vocal tuition", however, is our first fork in the process. This is where the changes we made to our To Be process mean that we are running two separate streams of the process concurrently. The paths of execution split up here and come back together at the "Contract supporting musicians" activity. Modeling this is pretty easy in jPDL. We start off by dropping a Fork node onto our process definition map, and joining it up to the previous node with a transition:

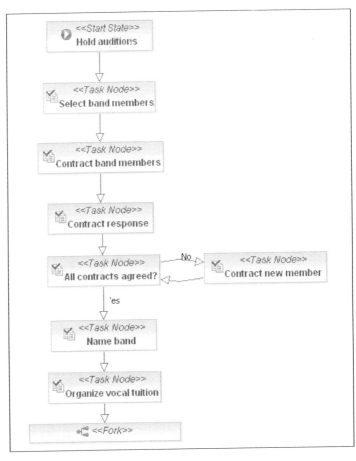

From here on, we just bring out two transitions from the fork and model our concurrent process paths as we usually would. Once all the nodes prior to "Contract supporting musicians" are in there, we simply bring the paths back together with two transitions coming into a Join node:

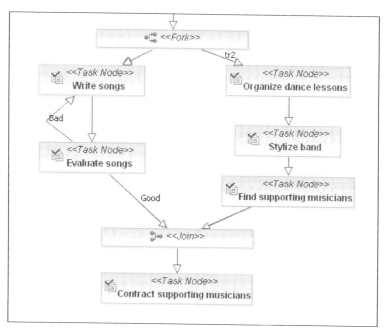

As you can see, we implemented another user decision task node for "Evaluate songs" in place of the "Songs are good?" decision box on the activity flow diagram. Other than that, the flow is very simple and there is nothing in there that we haven't already seen.

We are now on the downhill slope for this process: we've already completed all the more complex nodes. From here on in, the process is either very similar to what we have already seen, or it is even simpler to implement. For example, most of the remaining task nodes are implemented with a simple task plus a transition labeled "Done". If you imagine this in the user interface, all the end user will see is a task label of "*do this task*" then a button saying "Done" that they can click alongside the standard buttons of "Save" and "Cancel". We are therefore imagining that our diligent end user will go away, do the task, and then record in the system that they have completed what is asked of them, as well as perhaps recording a few details about their task in process variables. Quite often, however, we will merely reflect back to the end user the process variables that we have already captured as context for their task, using the read-only process variables that we have already input.

The end user can then select the "Done" transition to verify that they have completed the task and the process can move on to the next node:

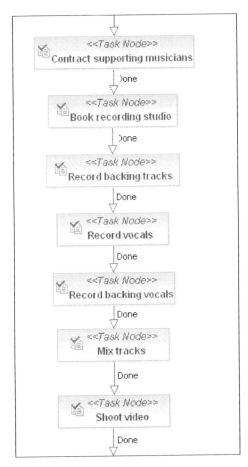

The rest of the process is very similar to what we've seen before. We do have another fork and join, which we implement in exactly the same way as we did before. We also do one more decision node, again implemented as a task node, where the human user inputs the outcome of the decision to choose the transition that is taken:

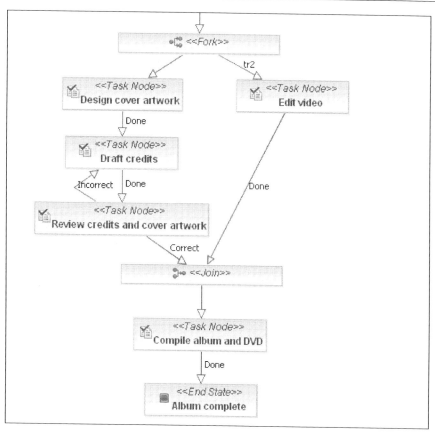

That really is all there is to it. Of course, we round off the process with an End node, but every other element of the process definition is something we have already seen. If you haven't already, take some time to import the process definition in the code download for this chapter and have a look through the nodes and XML to familiarize yourself with the structure.

Export for sign-off

So now we have completed our first iteration of the "Produce music products" process definition, all that remains is for us to obtain sign-off on our work so far. This is a simple matter of locating the `processimage.jpg` file and emailing it the sponsors to ask for sign-off. If your installation has followed the instructions in this chapter, then this can be found at the following location:

```
C:\MJC\Business Process Management\jBPM\jbpm-jpdl-3.2.GA\designer\
workspace\Bland Records\src\main\jpdl\Produce music products\
processimage.jpg
```

The final process map image file will look something like this:

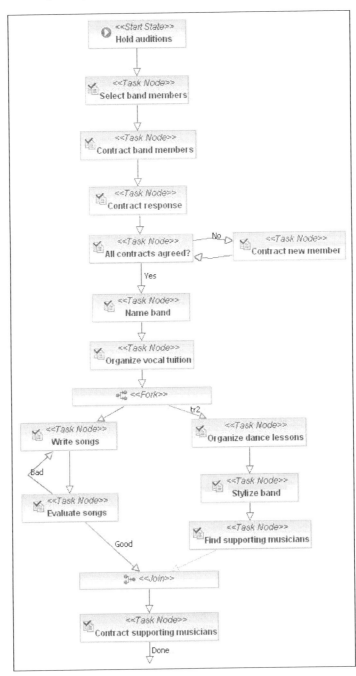

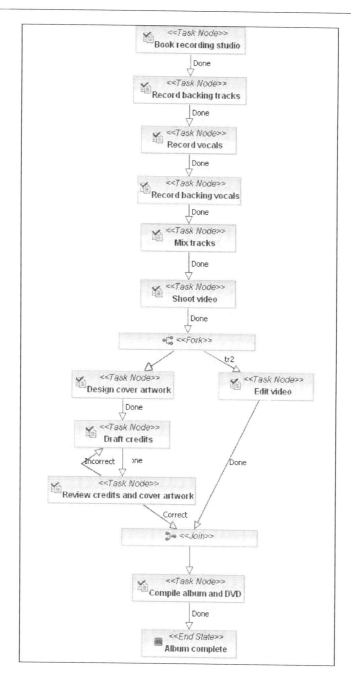

Once sign-off is obtained, we are now ready for the next stage, where we'll generate and adapt the user interface to the process that we have built in this chapter.

Summary

We have covered a great deal in this chapter, and we've come a long way. Let's just recap what we have been doing:

- We installed Java, the JBoss application server, the jBPM engine, and the jBPM Designer.
- We looked at the fundamental concepts that underpin JBoss jBPM.
- We put these concepts into practice by building our first process definition for our proof-of-concept system.

In the next chapter, we will take this to the next stage by taking a look at how the process definition we have built will look in the web console user interface.

4

The Prototype user interface

It's all very well having a beautiful process definition, but this is "business process management", not "business process definition". Having a process definition that accurately reflects the way the business works is only half the story. In this chapter, we'll add the majority of the remaining half. The final icing on the cake will be added in the last few chapters.

In this chapter, we are going to build the end user part of our BPM system. We will put together the user interface, which our proof-of-concept testers will use to interact with the process definition that we created in the previous chapter. By the end of the chapter, we will have obtained sign-off from our sponsors and the proof-of-concept testers indicating that they are happy that this user interface is ready to test. In the next chapter, we'll run our testing to prove that our BPM concept system will indeed meet Bland Records' requirements and should be further developed.

In this chapter, we will look at the following:

- Building web forms for the tasks we defined
- Setting up our proof-of-concept users in the system
- Deploying the process
- The default jBPM web console interface
- Adding some help text to the web console interface
- Obtaining sign-off that the web console is ready to run the proof of concept

Build the prototype

With the process engine of our BPM system now in place, it's time to turn our attention to the user interface that our users will interact with, as they execute the process. We will make this available over the internet as a series of web screens that the user can use like a regular website: the jBPM project refers to this as the "web console". For the time being, we will build the web console on our local machine, where we'll be able to play around with it until we are happy.

In the next chapter, we'll see how we can deploy it on a server, so our proof-of-concept users can test the system properly.

The web console is a combination of task lists, which represent the queue of work that a user or a group of users has to do, and task forms, which are the screens where the user can actually complete the tasks that have been assigned to them. As we'll see later in the chapter, the jBPM web console also comes with some other handy utilities out of the box, although most of these are more useful for management and administrators than end users.

Develop the prototype user interface

The first step is to build what jBPM terms the "task forms". These are the screens where the user will do the work assigned to them, making an update to a process variable or confirming they have done a piece of offline work, for example:

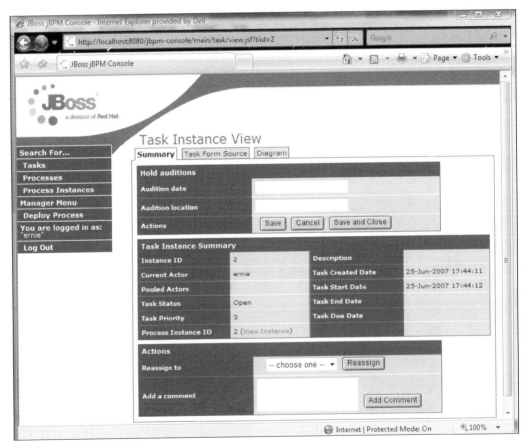

We need to generate one of these task forms for every task node in our process. This is quite a simple thing to do but, as there isn't a "generate all task forms" button, it is rather time consuming. Still, it does give us the opportunity to ensure each task form is correctly put together. The task forms use XHTML JavaServer Faces tags. JavaServer Faces (JSF) is a Java-based web application framework that simplifies the development of user interfaces for Java applications. For those who know some HTML, the syntax for the Faces tags is not a million miles away. For our purposes, we won't need to worry too much about the Faces elements, as we will limit our interaction with them to a few simple amendments and additions. Nevertheless, for those who are interested, there is a good tutorial on JavaServer Faces here:

```
http://www.exadel.com/tutorial/jsf/jsftutorial-kickstart.html
```

Anyway, on with our work. Start up the process Designer if you haven't already got it open. Highlight the first task node in the process diagram, which is of course our start node, "Hold auditions". In the Outline view, expand the tree until you find the "Hold auditions" task (note you need the task element within the node, not the node itself). Right-click and select **Properties**. In the left-hand menu, navigate to the **Advanced** screen. On here, you will see a **Generate Form...** button; click it:

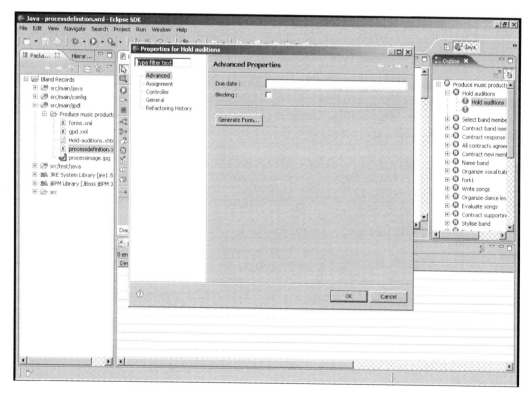

Once you've clicked to create the task form, the Designer will ask you to confirm the variables that you've already defined in the process definition and which should be collected on this task form. In our case, these are `audDate` and `audLocation` for the "Hold auditions" task node:

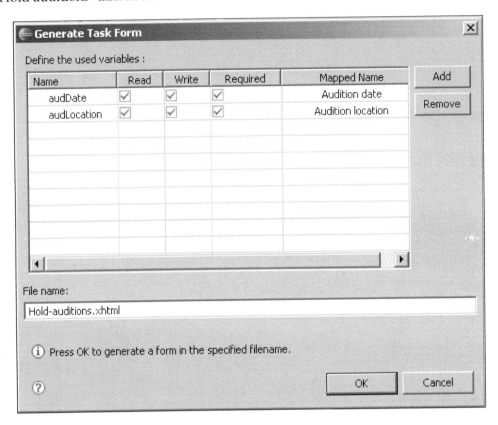

As mentioned in the previous chapter, it will be the mapped names of "Audition date" and "Audition location" that will actually be used in the web console, making for a more user-friendly experience.

You will notice at the bottom of this dialog window that the Designer automatically gives the task form file a name of `task node name.xhtml`, with `.xhtml` being the filename extension used for XHTML JavaServer Faces files. We should leave these settings as they are: the only time we'd need to change the filename is if we have two nodes called the same thing. Click **OK**, then **OK** again, to close the task node properties window and you will see in the Package Explorer window that the new task form file has been added to our project, along with an XML file called `forms.xml`:

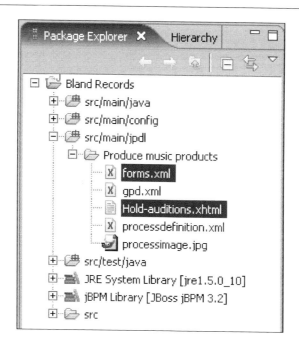

Double-click the `Hold-auditions.xhtml` file, so we can have a look at what's been created for us. Something like the following code should open up in the main editor window:

```
<!DOCTYPE html PUBLIC "-//W3C//DTD XHTML 1.0 Transitional//EN"
"http://www.w3.org/TR/xhtml1/DTD/xhtml1-transitional.dtd" >

<!-- the DOCTYPE means we are required to use html for a root element
-->
<html xmlns="http://www.w3.org/1999/xhtml"
      xmlns:ui="http://java.sun.com/jsf/facelets"
      xmlns:c="http://java.sun.com/jstl/core"
      xmlns:h="http://java.sun.com/jsf/html"
      xmlns:f="http://java.sun.com/jsf/core"
      xmlns:tf="http://jbpm.org/jsf/tf"
      xmlns:jbpm="http://jbpm.org/jsf">

  <ui:component>

    <jbpm:dataform>

      <f:facet name="header">
        <h:outputText value="#{taskName}"/>
      </f:facet>

      <!-- TASKFORM ROWS -->
```

```
<jbpm:datacell>
  <f:facet name="header">
      <h:outputText value="Audition date"/>
  </f:facet>
<h:inputText value="#{var['audDate']}" />
</jbpm:datacell>
<jbpm:datacell>
  <f:facet name="header">
      <h:outputText value="Audition location"/>
  </f:facet>
<h:inputText value="#{var['audLocation']}" />
</jbpm:datacell>

<jbpm:datacell>
  <f:facet name="header">
    <h:outputText value="Actions"/>
  </f:facet>
  <!-- TASKFORM BUTTONS -->
  <tf:saveButton value="Save"/>
  <tf:cancelButton value="Cancel"/>
  <tf:transitionButton value="Save and Close"/>
</jbpm:datacell>

</jbpm:dataform>

</ui:component>

</html>
```

As you can see, this code really isn't massively different from HTML: it is certainly pretty understandable to the uninitiated. Still, we don't actually have to worry about its content in any respect: we can quite happily leave it completely alone. Nevertheless, a bit later in this chapter, we will make a couple of edits to it, just to tailor it to our needs somewhat.

While we're here, we may as well have a quick look at the `forms.xml` file: double-click it to inspect it in the main editor window. The content in the **Source** view will be something like this:

```
<?xml version="1.0" encoding="UTF-8"?>

<forms>
  <form task="Hold auditions" form="Hold-auditions.xhtml"/>
</forms>
```

As you can see, this file is extremely simple and all it does is list out all the task forms that will be needed by the web console to execute the process definition. We will not need to edit this file at all.

Now comes the laborious bit: we must go into every task node that we have defined and repeat the above task form creation process. There should be no need to change any of the variables or file names, just accept the defaults that the Designer gives you. Obviously, you don't create any task forms for fork or join nodes, only for task nodes. When we've finished, we should have a long list of XHTML task form files in our Package Explorer:

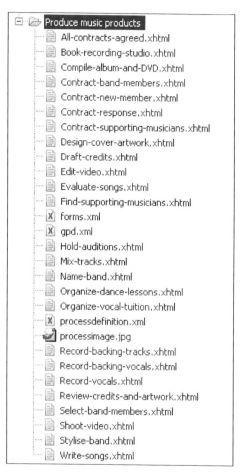

If you look at the XHTML code for a node where we have specified a name for a transition from the node, there will be a task form button tag included that will be called the same name as the transition. For example, in our Contract-supporting-musicians.xhtml task form, we have the following buttons specified:

```
<!-- TASKFORM BUTTONS -->
<tf:saveButton value="Save"/>
<tf:cancelButton value="Cancel"/>
<tf:transitionButton transition="Done" value="Done"/>
```

The `transitionButton` is given a value of "Done", the same name as the transition we specified, and will result in a button labeled "Done" showing up in the web console for our users to click. So even though the user won't actually input any process variables on this screen, they will move the process on by clicking the appropriately-labeled "Done" button to confirm they have done the task offline and the process can resume. Of course, this gets even more useful where we have specified two transitions and the task form will therefore include two buttons for the user to choose from. For example, the user will be able to choose between an "Incorrect" and a "Correct" button on the "Review credits and cover artwork" task form, because the Designer has automatically recognized that there are two leaving transitions and created the necessary buttons with the following code:

```
<!-- TASKFORM BUTTONS -->
<tf:saveButton value="Save"/>
<tf:cancelButton value="Cancel"/>
<tf:transitionButton transition="Incorrect" value="Incorrect"/>
<tf:transitionButton transition="Correct" value="Correct"/>
```

This is very clever stuff and goes to prove just how much jBPM is doing for us without us having to get our hands dirty with code.

Set up our users

By default, jBPM is set up with a few test users who happen to be characters from Sesame Street: Ernie, Grover, and so on. Unless we want to give our brave testers a complex, we had better set them up with some proper usernames for the system. Of course, these usernames have to have a correspondence with the swimlanes that we used in the previous chapter to assign tasks. The relationship is one of "users" belonging to "groups" and it is modeled in the database that underpins jBPM. The behavior we are looking for is that when Jack Thompson, who is a Talent Scout, logs into the web console, he should see tasks in his task list relating to "Hold auditions", as he fulfils the swimlane criteria for that node in our process definition. We can set up new users by copying in our group and user information to the pre-existing database tables.

We don't need to set up every single user in the organization right now, only those people who will be helping us out with testing our proof-of-concept system. We'll need at least one user for each type of swimlane. We'll give our users suitable, system-ready usernames, without any spaces or non-standard characters: this will make the upgrade path to fully integrate with a Windows domain easier in the long run. One consideration we do have to bear in mind: at run time, we won't know who some of our users will be, as they are actually defined during process execution. For example, we don't know who our band members are going to be until we've held auditions and selected the band. We can get round this by simply creating anonymous logins that whoever gets picked can use.

For our purposes, we'll set up the following groups and users:

- Talent scout — powellb
- Legal adviser — rumpoleh
- Band member — memberb
- Record producer — dredr
- Artist development — harrisr
- Songwriter — lennonj
- Musician — hendrixj
- Video production — welleso
- Artist — monetc
- Administrator — admin
- Manager — manager

In order to insert these users we need to get the database running. Start the JBoss application server with the shortcut we created in the last chapter. Once the application server has finished its start up routine, open up your web browser and go to `http://localhost:8080/jmx-console/`:

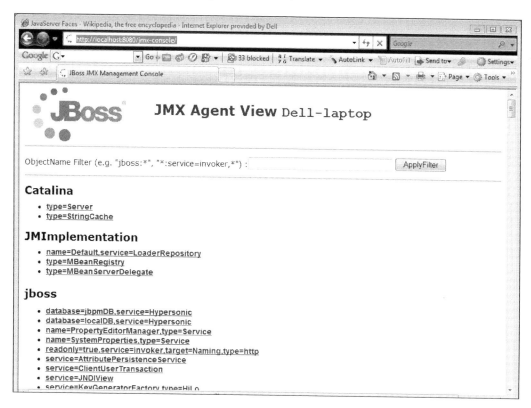

This is the management console that comes with the JBoss application server, which provides some utilities for managing it, including a simple database utility. We'll use this database utility to make the changes that we need. The database used in the default jBPM installation is called Hypersonic: it is a perfectly reasonable database for testing out jBPM on our local machine, although, in a later chapter, we'll see how we can swap it for a more robust database when we want to use our BPM system in anger.

In the JMX Console, under the **jboss** heading you will see a link entitled **database=jbpmDB, service=Hypersonic**: click this link. Scroll down the next page until you get to a line called **void startDatabaseManager()**. Click the **Invoke** button directly underneath. You will go to a new screen and after a few moments' delay the HSQL Database Manager will start:

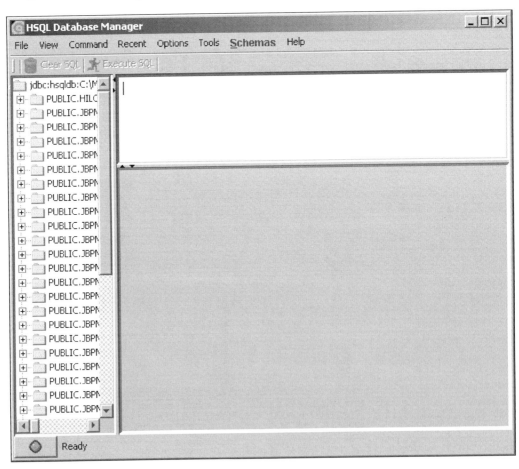

On the left of the Database Manager, you can see the list of all the database tables used by jBPM. The tables we are interested in are PUBLIC.JBPM_ID_GROUP, PUBLIC.JBPM_ID_MEMBERSHIP, and PUBLIC.JBPM_ID_USER. If you want to see the existing contents of these tables, you can type this simple bit of SQL into the cursor window at the top and click **Execute SQL**:

```
SELECT * FROM PUBLIC.JBPM_ID_GROUP
```

This will bring back the list of groups that are already set up in jBPM. As you can see there are five columns in the table: ID_, CLASS_, NAME_, TYPE_, and PARENT_. We won't linger over the meaning of these columns; suffice it to say that the values in these columns define the relationships between the database tables that manage jBPM users. We need to add our own groups in, and again, we do this by running a bit of SQL on the database. You can either type the following in yourself or copy and paste in the code from the insert-groups.sql file that is in the code download for this chapter:

```
/*First we add in the security roles*/
INSERT INTO PUBLIC.JBPM_ID_GROUP VALUES (301,'G','manager','security-
role',NULL)
INSERT INTO PUBLIC.JBPM_ID_GROUP VALUES (302,'G','participant','securi
ty-role',NULL)
INSERT INTO PUBLIC.JBPM_ID_GROUP VALUES (303,'G','administrator','secu
rity-role',NULL)

/*Then we add in the organisations*/
INSERT INTO PUBLIC.JBPM_ID_GROUP VALUES (201,'G','Talent scout','organ
isation',NULL)
INSERT INTO PUBLIC.JBPM_ID_GROUP VALUES (202,'G','Legal adviser','orga
nisation',NULL)
INSERT INTO PUBLIC.JBPM_ID_GROUP VALUES (203,'G','Band member','organ
isation',NULL)
INSERT INTO PUBLIC.JBPM_ID_GROUP VALUES (204,'G','Record producer','or
ganisation',NULL)
INSERT INTO PUBLIC.JBPM_ID_GROUP VALUES (205,'G','Artist development',
'organisation',NULL)
INSERT INTO PUBLIC.JBPM_ID_GROUP VALUES (206,'G','Songwriter','organi
sation',NULL)
INSERT INTO PUBLIC.JBPM_ID_GROUP VALUES (207,'G','Musician','organisa
tion',NULL)
INSERT INTO PUBLIC.JBPM_ID_GROUP VALUES (208,'G','Video production','o
rganisation',NULL)
INSERT INTO PUBLIC.JBPM_ID_GROUP VALUES (209,'G','Artist','organisati
on',NULL)
INSERT INTO PUBLIC.JBPM_ID_GROUP VALUES (210,'G','Administrator','orga
nisation',NULL)
INSERT INTO PUBLIC.JBPM_ID_GROUP VALUES (211,'G','Manager','organisat
ion',NULL)
```

After you click the **Execute SQL** button, the Database Manager should come back with confirmation that the new groups have been added:

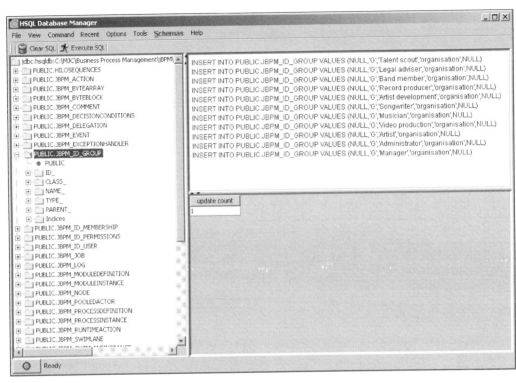

If you run the SELECT * FROM PUBLIC.JBPM_ID_GROUP command again, you will see that our new groups are now in the table:

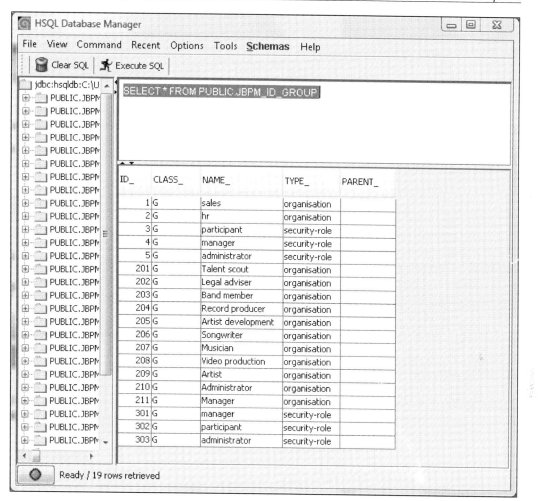

Now we need to do another insert for our new users:

```
INSERT INTO PUBLIC.JBPM_ID_USER VALUES (101,'U','powellb','powellb@
bland.com','powellb')
INSERT INTO PUBLIC.JBPM_ID_USER VALUES (102,'U','rumpoleh','rumpoleh@
bland.com','rumpoleh')
INSERT INTO PUBLIC.JBPM_ID_USER VALUES (103,'U','memberb','memberb@
bland.com','memberb')
INSERT INTO PUBLIC.JBPM_ID_USER VALUES (104,'U','dredr','dredr@bland.
com','dredr')
INSERT INTO PUBLIC.JBPM_ID_USER VALUES (105,'U','harrisr','harrisr@
bland.com','harrisr')
```

```
INSERT INTO PUBLIC.JBPM_ID_USER VALUES (106,'U','lennonj','lennonj@
bland.com','lennonj')
INSERT INTO PUBLIC.JBPM_ID_USER VALUES (107,'U','hendrixj','hendrixj@
bland.com','hendrixj')
INSERT INTO PUBLIC.JBPM_ID_USER VALUES (108,'U','welleso','welleso@
bland.com','welleso')
INSERT INTO PUBLIC.JBPM_ID_USER VALUES (109,'U','monetc','monetc@
bland.com','monetc')
INSERT INTO PUBLIC.JBPM_ID_USER VALUES (110,'U','admin','admin@bland.
com','admin')
INSERT INTO PUBLIC.JBPM_ID_USER VALUES (111,'U','manager','manager@
bland.com','manager')
```

Again, you can either type in the command yourself or use the `insert-users.sql` file in the code download. Finally, we have to link our users to our groups through the PUBLIC.JBPM_ID_MEMBERSHIP table. We need to define all our users with a security role of "participant". In addition, our Administrator is given security roles of both "administrator" and "manager", and our Manager has a security role of "manager". We also need to assign each user to the swimlane groups that we have just added to the database. We do this by adding in new rows to the PUBLIC.JBPM_ID_MEMBERSHIP table, specifying the relationships between the rows in the PUBLIC.JBPM_ID_USER and PUBLIC.JBPM_ID_GROUP tables. We link the two tables' ID fields together: if you have deviated from the standard installation in any way, you will have to edit the following SQL to get the relationships right as specified above:

```
/*Then we make all our normal users participants*/
INSERT INTO PUBLIC.JBPM_ID_MEMBERSHIP VALUES (NULL,'M',NULL,NULL,'101
','302')
INSERT INTO PUBLIC.JBPM_ID_MEMBERSHIP VALUES (NULL,'M',NULL,NULL,'102
','302')
INSERT INTO PUBLIC.JBPM_ID_MEMBERSHIP VALUES (NULL,'M',NULL,NULL,'103
','302')
INSERT INTO PUBLIC.JBPM_ID_MEMBERSHIP VALUES (NULL,'M',NULL,NULL,'104
','302')
INSERT INTO PUBLIC.JBPM_ID_MEMBERSHIP VALUES (NULL,'M',NULL,NULL,'105
','302')
INSERT INTO PUBLIC.JBPM_ID_MEMBERSHIP VALUES (NULL,'M',NULL,NULL,'106
','302')
INSERT INTO PUBLIC.JBPM_ID_MEMBERSHIP VALUES (NULL,'M',NULL,NULL,'107
','302')
INSERT INTO PUBLIC.JBPM_ID_MEMBERSHIP VALUES (NULL,'M',NULL,NULL,'108
','302')
```

```
INSERT INTO PUBLIC.JBPM_ID_MEMBERSHIP VALUES (NULL,'M',NULL,NULL,'109
','302')

INSERT INTO PUBLIC.JBPM_ID_MEMBERSHIP VALUES (NULL,'M',NULL,NULL,'110
','302')
INSERT INTO PUBLIC.JBPM_ID_MEMBERSHIP VALUES (NULL,'M',NULL,NULL,'111
','302')

/*Then we make the administrator an administrator*/
INSERT INTO PUBLIC.JBPM_ID_MEMBERSHIP VALUES (NULL,'M',NULL,NULL,'110
','303')

/*Then we make the manager and the administrator a manager*/
INSERT INTO PUBLIC.JBPM_ID_MEMBERSHIP VALUES (NULL,'M',NULL,NULL,'111
','301')
INSERT INTO PUBLIC.JBPM_ID_MEMBERSHIP VALUES (NULL,'M',NULL,NULL,'110
','301')

/*Finally we add all our users to their organisation groups*/
INSERT INTO PUBLIC.JBPM_ID_MEMBERSHIP VALUES (NULL,'M',NULL,NULL,'101
','201')
INSERT INTO PUBLIC.JBPM_ID_MEMBERSHIP VALUES (NULL,'M',NULL,NULL,'102
','202')
INSERT INTO PUBLIC.JBPM_ID_MEMBERSHIP VALUES (NULL,'M',NULL,NULL,'103
','203')
INSERT INTO PUBLIC.JBPM_ID_MEMBERSHIP VALUES (NULL,'M',NULL,NULL,'104
','204')
INSERT INTO PUBLIC.JBPM_ID_MEMBERSHIP VALUES (NULL,'M',NULL,NULL,'105
','205')
INSERT INTO PUBLIC.JBPM_ID_MEMBERSHIP VALUES (NULL,'M',NULL,NULL,'106
','206')
INSERT INTO PUBLIC.JBPM_ID_MEMBERSHIP VALUES (NULL,'M',NULL,NULL,'107
','207')
INSERT INTO PUBLIC.JBPM_ID_MEMBERSHIP VALUES (NULL,'M',NULL,NULL,'108
','208')
INSERT INTO PUBLIC.JBPM_ID_MEMBERSHIP VALUES (NULL,'M',NULL,NULL,'109
','209')
```

Phew, thankfully that's done, our proof-of-concept users are set up and ready to go. We can now safely close the Database Manager.

Deploy the process and user interface

Let's now deploy our process definition and console task forms to the server, so we can have a play around with them. First, start the application server again, if you closed it after the database changes we just made. Next, in the Designer, switch to the Deployment tab of the main editing window. You will be presented with a list of all the files that are available for deployment to the application server:

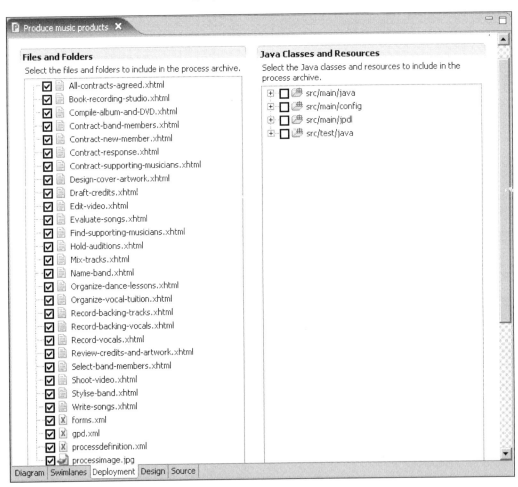

Make sure that all of the files in the left-hand pane are checked: by default, the files in the right-hand pane will be unchecked and we can leave it that way for now. In later chapters, we'll see how to deploy Java classes and resources through the right-hand pane. Scrolling down, we can see that we also have the opportunity here to specify the URL of the application server to which we should deploy our files:

Local Save Settings

Choose if and where you wish to save the process archive locally.

☐ Save Process Archive Locally

Location: [   ] [Search...]

[Save Without Deploying...]

Deployment Server Settings

Specify the settings of the server you wish to deploy to.

Server Name: [localhost]

Server Port: [8080]

Server Deployer: [/jbpm-console/upload]

[Test Connection...]

[Deploy Process Archive...]

It shouldn't be necessary to change the settings here, although, it is worthwhile clicking the **Test Connection** button to make sure the Designer can connect to the application server without any problems. If all is well, click the **Deploy Process Archive** button to deploy our files to the application server. This is all we need to do to put our process live.

One nice little feature of jBPM is that the engine is smart enough to keep track of the versions of our process that we deploy, without us having to manually provide version numbers or worry about overwriting previous versions of the process. For example, if I open up the Database Manager again and look in the PUBLIC. JBPM_PROCESSDEFINITION table at the versions of our "Produce music products" process that I have deployed to the application server I can see eight versions:

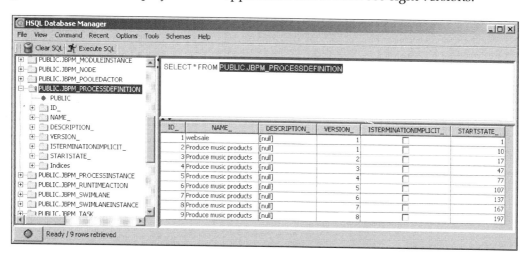

Every time I click the **Deploy Process Archive** button, a new version of the "Produce music products" process is added to the end of this table.

Investigating the web console interface

The jBPM web console is where our users will do their tasks, monitor the process, and administer the running of the live process. The web console is developed and maintained by the jBPM project team as an example of a web front-end to the jBPM process engine. The intention is that the example web console can serve as the starting point for jBPM users' own implementations of jBPM: it can be developed and tailored to our exact needs. Of course, if you do make improvements and develop the code base, you should submit your changes back to the jBPM community to help make the project even better.

At the time of writing, the web console is under very active development for the 3.2 release of jBPM, and hence the version that you actually end up using may well differ slightly from that presented in these pages. No matter, the concepts will remain the same and it will only be aesthetic differences, if there are any.

Let's have a look at the web console. With the application server running, fire up your browser and go to `http://localhost:8080/jbpm-console/` where you will be presented with the console login page:

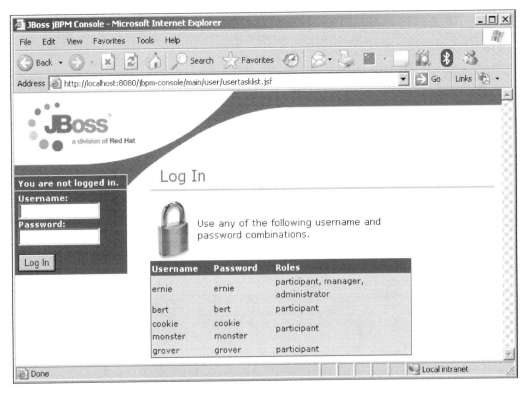

In the middle of the screen, there is a hard-coded table featuring the usernames that are used with the default jBPM example process. We can ignore these and use one of our own logins that we put into the database, previously. Log in with the username and password of "powellb" and "powellb", to log in as our Talent scout. Once we're logged in, we can see the various portions of the web console that we can interact with, some of which are targeted at end users, some at managers, and some at administrators:

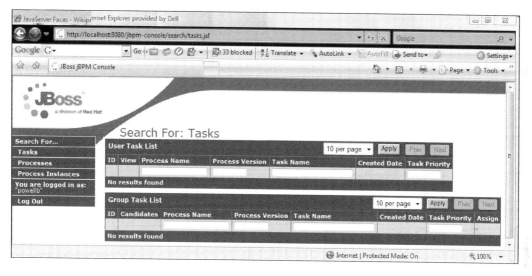

Of course, in a live environment we'd probably want to change this a bit so that end users don't get to see the managerial or administration sections, but we won't worry about that for now. Let's explore the various parts of the console. To make our exploration meaningful, let's create an instance of our process. Click **Processes**, then **Start process** next to the latest version of the "Produce music products" process:

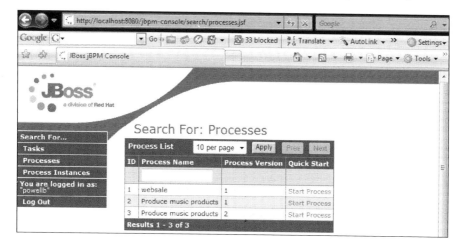

This starts a new instance of the process and takes us to the first task form. If you now click **Process Instances**, you will see a list of all instances of the process that are currently in course on this server. If you click **View** you can see all the details of that process instance:

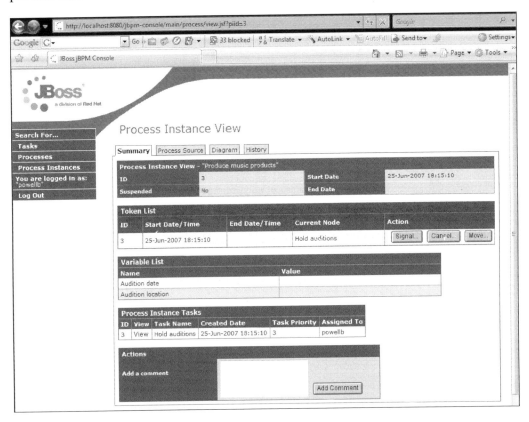

From here, we can inspect the process definition diagram and code, as well as see some history of what has happened to this instance of the process while it has been running.

End users

End users will naturally be the heaviest users of the process's user interface, and there are two elements of the web console, in particular, that are expressly designed for them: tasks lists and task forms. The ordinary user should live and breathe in their task list as it represents the queue of work that they have to complete to fulfil their part of the process.

The web console actually contains two task lists, one for the user, but also one for the group. The user's task list presents a list of all the tasks that are currently assigned to the user that is logged in. For example, if we click **User Task List** in the menu we can see that we currently have one task assigned to us:

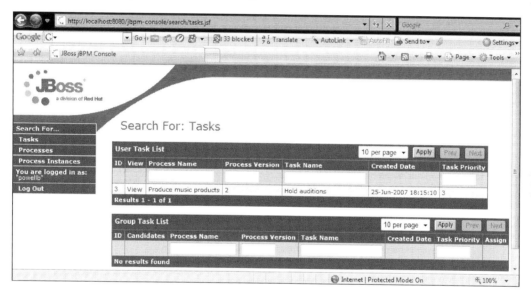

This makes sense as we are currently logged in as a Talent scout, and we have just started an instance of the process where the first task node, "Hold auditions", is assigned to the Talent scout swimlane. If you were to log out and log in as a different user, you would see that their task list is currently empty, as they haven't had anything assigned to them yet.

You will also notice as you play around with the web console that tasks exist in either the user task list or the group task list, but not both. This is to make sure that you don't get multiple users working on the same group task: the idea is that the user "takes" a task off the group stack and adds it to their own to work on it. The group task list is intended for situations where you have a pool of users, any one of whom could take the task, removing it from the group task list and bringing it into their personal user task list.

If we go back to the user task list, and click View, next to the task we have assigned to us in our list, we are presented with the screens we need to be able to complete this task. This is the task form we generated previously, and we can now see how those XHTML elements are rendered in our browser:

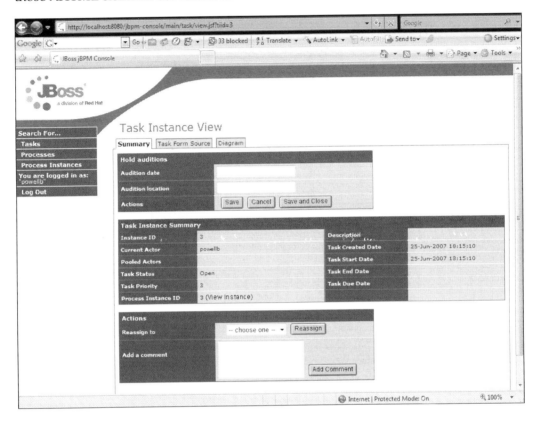

We can see that the web console has indeed picked up the "mapped names" of our process variables, using "Audition date" and "Audition location" as the labels in the input form. We can also see that the task form has three action buttons that the user can click: **Save**, **Cancel**, and **Save and Close**. The **Save** and **Cancel** buttons will be present on every task form page, although we will find that later in the process the **Save and Close** button will be called different things. This is because this button is the `transitionButton` element we saw earlier that will pick up the transition name, if one is specified. If there isn't a name specified for the transition, the button is simply labeled **End Task** by default. The **Save** button allows the user to fill out the task form and save its contents without submitting it and moving to the next node of the process. This is particularly useful in more complex forms where the user may not know exactly what they need to enter straight off. Similarly, the **Cancel** button allows the user to discard any input that they have made and go back to their task list without moving on in the process.

One of the best features of the web console, one which really highlights the benefits of business process management, is shown in the **Diagram** tab of the task form:

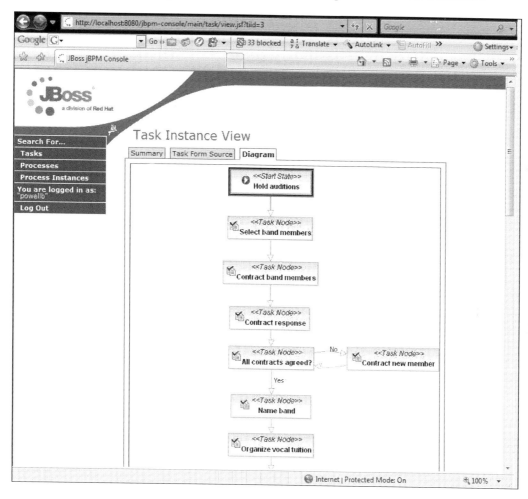

As you can see, this screen shows the user how their current task fits into the context of the process as a whole, by highlighting the current node in the process diagram. This is incredibly powerful from an end user's point of view as they can easily see how they are one cog in a bigger machine, and how the quality and timeliness of their work affects the work of others.

If we go back to the task form, enter some example data into the form and click **End Task,** the process variables we have entered are saved to the jBPM database, the task is marked as completed and the process execution moves on to the next node in the process definition. As the next task node is also assigned to our Talent scout, we can go back into the task list and pick up the next task:

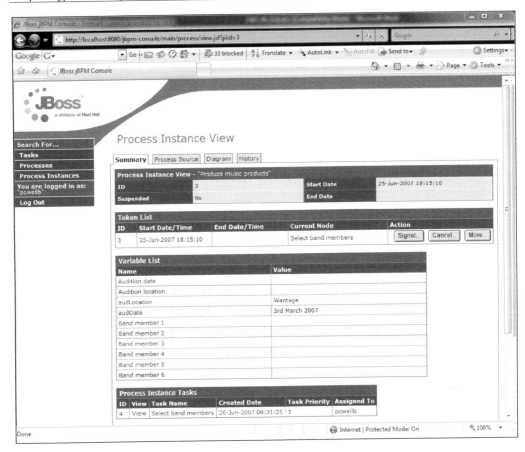

Managers

The managerial part of the web console is probably the least developed part of the system at the moment. It is anticipated that managers will be able to use the web console to deploy new processes, monitor operation of the process, correct end users' process variable mistakes, cancel processes if need be, and monitor process timers. However, this functionality hasn't been fully developed at the time of writing: perhaps it will have been by the time you come to read this book. Nevertheless, never fear, as some of this functionality overlaps with the Business Activity Monitoring functionality that we will build in a later chapter.

If you log out of the web console and log back in with the username "manager" and password "manager", you can see that there is one more menu option available to our managers, "Deploy process":

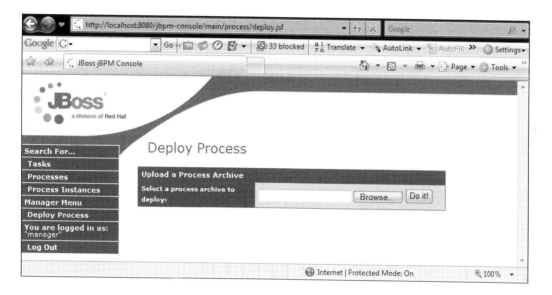

This is actually an alternative way for us to deploy our processes, rather than using the deployment functionality in the Designer. Personally, I find it easier to use the Designer's deployer, but you might want to experiment with this one.

Of course, managers can also go into any of the task forms through the Process instances menu and use the re-assignment functionality to re-distribute the workload around their team:

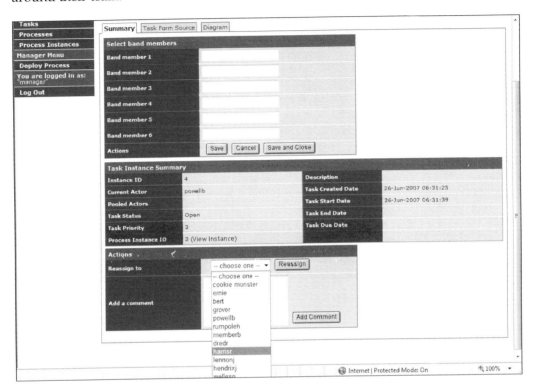

Adapt the web console

The web console functions perfectly well as it is, although there are obviously a few things we'd like to do to make it our own. In later chapters, we'll make some further adaptations to the web console, but for now we'll content ourselves with adding some "help" text to the task form pages to give our proof-of-concept testers a few pointers as to how they should use the system. We are simply going to include a bit of text on each task form telling the users what is expected of them. We can do this with some very straightforward HTML. Go back into the Designer and double-click the `hold-auditions.xhtml` task form in the Package Explorer. Scroll down to the end of the code and add the following lines of HTML and text on a new line between the `dataform` and `uicomponent` closing tags:

```
<br /><br />
   Add in the date and location of the next audition. Please enter the
date in the format DD-MM-YYYY.
```

```
<br /><br />
    When you've finished click Save to save your changes for later, or
click End Task to submit and move on. You can click Cancel if you
don't want to save your changes and are not ready to submit.
    <br /><br />
```

Hopefully, this code isn't too earth shattering for you. If we now re-deploy the process definition to the server, start a new instance of this latest version of the process and have a look at the Hold auditions task form, we can see that our help text shows up on the screen to help our users understand what they need to do:

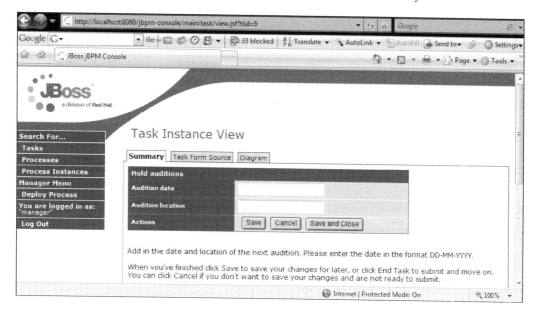

You can do this for every task form where you believe it would be worthwhile to give the end user a bit of a helping hand. Remember, however, that if for some reason you have to re-generate the task form your help text will be lost.

Sign off for the proof of concept

All that remains now is to demonstrate the proof-of-concept web console to the sponsor and the proof-of-concept testers, and to ask them to sign it off as ready for testing. At this stage, it is very worthwhile setting some expectations and making it clear to these people that they are not signing off the system as being production-ready, merely that the bare functionality is in place to have a meaningful proof-of-concept test.

We also need to ask our proof-of-concept users to start gathering together the data they will need to put the system through its paces. They should look at historical records of the process to pull together this information: although, sometimes there will be no option but to fake it as the data may not have been recorded. As long as the data is sensible and realistic, there is no problem with this approach. The important thing is that the process definition and the user interface can be tested under semi-realistic conditions by the testers going through the process in "fast forward" with pre-determined data.

Summary

In this chapter, we have built the user interface that our proof-of-concept testers will use to interact with the process definition, which we built in the previous chapter. At this stage, we are not worrying about making the web console look pretty or in adapting it for our specific requirements: we are just going to make do with what is available out of the box. After all, the basic functionality of the jBPM web console is actually quite advanced and really provides more than enough for us to get started. In later chapters, we'll tinker here and there with it and we'll work at making the system more production-ready. But for now, we have our proof-of-concept system ready to go, and in the next chapter we'll see if we can indeed prove that concept.

We have covered:

- Building task forms
- Setting up users and groups
- Deploying the process
- The elements of the user interface
- Adding help text to the task forms
- Obtaining sign-off that the UI is ready to run the proof of concept

Our final deliverable from this phase has been the web console that has been signed off as fit for the purposes of running our proof of concept test.

5
Iterate the prototype

Having built our prototype, we must put it in front of some users for some preliminary testing. This is our "proof-of-concept" stage. This is really our last chance to throw out our BPM system before we commit to it and go forward with an implementation. We need to put it through its paces, and work out whether or not it is going to fit the bill for what we need from it.

In this chapter, we will cover:

- Setting up the proof of concept
- Making the prototype available on a server
- Running the proof-of-concept test
- Making changes to the process
- Integrating with other systems

By the end of this chapter, we will have obtained sign-off from our sponsor that we are ready to move to full-scale user acceptance testing and implementation.

Set up for the proof of concept

It is important to get our proof of concept off on the right foot: a little bit of effort at the start will pay huge dividends further down the line. The most important thing we have to do is make it clear to everyone involved exactly what we are setting out to achieve.

Set up the team

Who do we want involved in our proof of concept? Well, everybody: or at least, a representative of each stakeholder group involved in the process. If we don't have full representation, then we might miss something and jeopardize the validity of the test. More crucially, those missing stakeholders would be well within their rights to withhold the sign-off and prevent us from progressing.

Full representation doesn't just mean a name on a sheet of paper, it means full participation in every aspect of the proof-of-concept program. The people who are seconded to the proof of concept must have the scope from their managers to step back from their day job, so that they can give us their full attention without distractions. Participants who aren't released from their day-to-day tasks won't give us 100% and again we risk losing our way.

Once the team is assembled and knows the level of commitment that is expected, we can set out the methodology that we intend to apply for the proof of concept.

Set expectations

Typically, we would expect a proof of concept to be started with a kick-off meeting to which all the protagonists are invited. At this meeting, we must set out with crystal clarity exactly what we will (and what we will not) achieve by running the proof of concept. It is vital that users understand we are not perfecting an almost-ready-for-go-live system, we are in the early stages of building a prototype. They must understand that prototypes are put together quickly to demonstrate whether or not a concept works, with scant regard for aesthetics, security, stability or any of the other things one expects from a production system.

So what are we trying to achieve? Some of it is about whether or not we have put the system together correctly, but it is also important we relate back to our original project objective, which if you remember, was as follows:

> **Project objective:** streamline the process as much as possible, and then implement a business process management system allowing Bland Records to better coordinate their suppliers and gain visibility of their pipeline.

So, in addition to considering how well what we have built achieves the above objective, we should also list out in the kick-off meeting the more system-related considerations:

- Does the process we've defined, fit with business reality?
- Is the user interface usable? Can we execute the process in its entirety?
- Does the support given by the system allow the process to run more smoothly?
- What needs to be added/changed/removed to improve the operation of the process?

Plan the proof-of-concept program

Any plan is about juggling the three pillars of project management: time, budget, and resources. We should build a plan for our proof of concept that sets out exactly what we intend in each of these three areas, given the things we need to achieve. Once we have the overall direction set, we need to break down the program into task-level activities with dates and milestones.

Before we get started, we need to make sure our stakeholders have gathered the data they will need to put the process through its paces. They need to look over old case files, emails, and so on to gather the data they are going to need: this task can easily be delegated to a working group drawn from the stakeholders themselves. At this stage, we should apply the Pareto principle and make sure we use the 20% of possible process scenarios that account for 80% of the work that actually goes through. We can look at the weird and wonderful exceptions to the process later: for now, let's just make sure the thing hangs together.

With the data in place, the team will be ready to start work. Daily review meetings are a good idea: they keep the team motivated and make sure everyone is moving in the same direction. Typically, a period of testing will be followed by a period of fix, followed by another period of testing. Weekly or bi-weekly iterations fit this pattern and can be reflected on the plan.

Capture requirements

We must make sure that we are ready to document and store the issues that our team comes up with when they start testing. The more effort we put into capturing these issues and requirements in a structured way, the better (it will make our lives easier in the long run when we try to prioritize and work on them).

If you are lucky enough to have a requirements management toolset in your organization, then this is an excellent opportunity to put it through its paces. Failing that, there are several relatively low-tech options available. A small Access database or a well-structured spreadsheet can quite easily do the job. With a team of users all potentially accessing and updating the same list of issues, it is important to lay down a few ground rules about versioning and concurrent access to avoid unfortunate mistakes. On recent projects, I have started using a Google Documents spreadsheet, shared with all the team members, with Google providing the versioning and concurrent access support: it's simple but it works.

In capturing the issues as they arise, we should force our users to pre-analyze the issues they are raising. For example, they can give us an indication of the seriousness of the issue, as well as giving us insight into any workarounds that exist.

This sort of information will help us to filter and prioritize the list of issues. An example structure might be:

- Reference:
- Issue short description:
- Issue detailed description:
- Logged by:
- Logged date:
- Severity (blocker/major/minor/optional):
- Workaround:

Then, with the addition of another few fields, this same list can also be used by the application team to log the work they have done on these issues.

- Status (open/rejected/resolved):
- Fix priority (high/medium/low):
- Fixer assigned:
- Comments:

For example, where the users have raised duplicate issues, the duplicates can be marked as "rejected". The remaining issues can then be prioritized for the next round of fixing, with comments added about what the potential fix might be. With the entire team working from the same list, we will have good communication and hopefully progress quickly.

Make jBPM available on a server

With our would-be users raring to go and with our plan in place, we had better make jBPM available to them so they can get cracking. We need to get the jBPM engine and the application server running on a server machine, so our users can access it and start testing. In many organizations, this work will be undertaken by a central IT department, and as the installation steps are exactly the same as we have already seen for getting it running on our local machine, we won't go over it again here. Once the software is installed and the database has been set up as described in the previous chapter, we will be ready to deploy our process. We should still be able to do this from our local machine, the intention of course, being that we can continue to develop the process locally and deploy to the remote server when we are happy with it.

Start up the Designer and go to the **Deployment** tab. In the **Deployment Server Settings** dialog, change the Server Name (and port if your IT department has changed the default port) to the name or IP address of the server where jBPM is installed. In our case, our server has an IP address of 192.168.2.3:

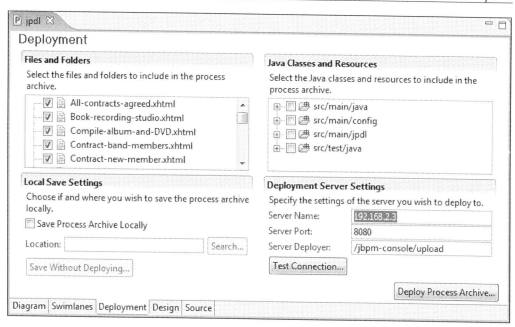

Test the connection and if all seems fine, click **Deploy Process Archive**.

If we now open up our browser and type in the URL for our jBPM console on the remote server, we should get our login page. In our example, we are connecting to our server from a Windows Vista machine:

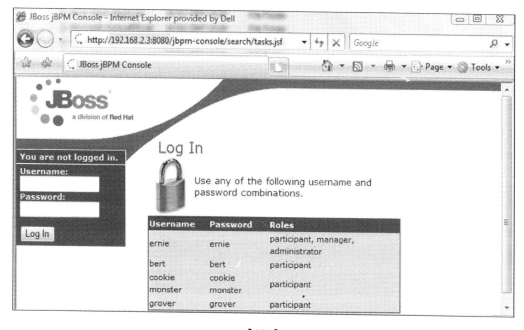

That's it, we're ready to go. In a later chapter, we'll see how we can make this server installation more robust by using a more scalable database back-end than the one that comes with jBPM by default, but for the purposes of our proof of concept the Hypersonic database will be just fine.

Run the proof of concept

With everything in place, we can get our team going on their testing. As issues come through, we can use the daily review meetings to make sure high quality information is logged and that prioritization is effective. We can also use this as a forum to challenge some of the process issues that come up: are the exceptions to the process really valid, or is this a once-in-a-lifetime event that we shouldn't be too concerned about? Quite often, we can expect to hear arguments such as "it has always worked that way" or "that's just the way it is". These aren't necessarily valid reasons for changing the process definition: each should be assessed on its own merits and we must try to diffuse the emotion that process change can bring about. It is vital that we get support from our project sponsor in these discussions: the sponsor should sign off on the justification for any changes.

Iterate the system

At the end of each testing period, we need to step back and assess our progress. Are the issues that are being raised related to the underlying process or to the web console user interface? The two types of issues would probably be worked on by different parts of the application team, so it would be good to make responsibility for each issue clear in the list.

It is also worthwhile looking at the results on a fundamental level: are the issues that are coming up ones that can be fixed, or is jBPM simply not the right kind of solution for our problem? We should not feel bad if indeed, we do have to reject jBPM, as there is no point flogging a dead horse, and sometimes, it is better to admit defeat than carry on regardless.

Process changes

By now you should be pretty comfortable with making changes to the process definition and redeploying. It should simply be a case of making the change to the process map, generating any task forms that might be needed, and deploying the process definition to the server. There are also some more advanced features of the jBPM Process Definition Language that we can also look at, trying them out here to see if they are useful.

Task prioritization

Not all tasks are created equal. Some tasks within the process are more important than others, and if your user has one in their task list, you want to make sure they complete that task as soon as possible. If we have a look at the user task list in the web console, we can see that there is a column devoted to **Task Priority**:

ID	View	Process Name	Process Version	Task Name	Created Date	Task Priority
6	View	Produce music products	2	Select band members	24-Feb-2007 15:58:42	3
8	View	Produce music products	2	Select band members	24-Feb-2007 15:59:12	3
9	View	Produce music products	2	Hold auditions	24-Feb-2007 15:59:18	3

User Task List — 10 per page — Apply — Prev — Next
Results 1 - 3 of 3

Now, while this functionality doesn't drive anything very special, it does allow our users to quickly get a handle on the tasks in their task list that they should do first.

We can set our tasks to the most appropriate priority when designing the process. We need to look at the XML definition of the task in the **Source** view of the process in the Designer. All we need to do is find the task in question, and add an attribute of `priority=""`, and then in between the quotation marks, we put a number between 1 and 5, with 1 being the highest priority and 5 the lowest. If we do this for our "Hold auditions" task, we end up with a task definition looking like this:

```
<task name="Hold auditions" swimlane="Talent scout" priority="1">
    <controller>
        <variable name="audDate" access="read,write,required"
mapped-name="Audition date"></variable>
        <variable name="audLocation" access="read,write,required"
mapped-name="Audition location"></variable>
    </controller>
</task>
```

If we now re-deploy the process definition and start an instance of the process, we'll see that powellb ends up with a task in their task list with a priority of "1":

ID	View	Process Name	Process Version	Task Name	Created Date	Task Priority
6	View	Produce music products	2	Select band members	24-Feb-2007 15:58:42	3
8	View	Produce music products	2	Select band members	24-Feb-2007 15:59:12	3
9	View	Produce music products	2	Hold auditions	24-Feb-2007 15:59:18	3
10	View	Produce music products	3	Hold auditions	24-Feb-2007 16:15:42	1

User Task List — 10 per page — Apply — Prev — Next
Results 1 - 4 of 4

Now they'll know they have to do this task first. When this is done for every task in the process definition, the end result is quite powerful and should certainly help our users be more productive.

Integration with other systems

In the vast majority of situations business processes involve the use of one or more IT systems. Our jBPM implementation is not necessarily trying to replace these systems; rather our goal is to coordinate their use. Nevertheless, there are opportunities where instead of our user getting a task in jBPM, and then going away to a separate system to complete the task, we might be able to do the task directly from the jBPM user interface.

Obviously, this has great benefits in terms of time saving and the user experience, although we should clearly bear in mind the maintenance overhead that may come about as a result of building this interface. We would most commonly build an interface such as this where we want to "wrapper" a legacy system that works well, but is no longer actively developed: quite often invoicing, warehousing, and other back-office applications fall into this category. We may also want to store some of the data that we are using in our process in a data warehousing application, as it may be of strategic use beyond the confines of our process. Not only can we interface to our own in-house applications, we might also want to interface directly with those of our suppliers, so we can get the whole supply chain moving smoothly.

Normally, this would be work undertaken by the developers on our application team, but as the concept is a general one and it helps us as BAs to understand what's involved, we will go through a very simple example here. We should also bear in mind that we wouldn't typically advocate doing complex system integrations during the proof-of-concept stage of the project.

All we will do here is push some of our process data into an external database to prove that we can do it. Our example business scenario will be that we have a royalties application, which another part of the business uses to pay songwriters whatever they are due on publication of their songs. We will therefore take the songwriters' names and the names of their songs, and put them into the back-end database of this putative royalties application.

In order to prove this concept, we have installed a MySQL 4.1 database on a server on our network and set up a database called `royalties`, with a table called `songs`. We have also installed a MySQL driver on our jBPM server that will help jBPM connect to the MySQL database. In order to do this, go here and download the driver: `http://www.mysql.com/downloads/api-jdbc.html`. Put the downloaded `.jar` file into the `lib` folder of your JBoss server installation; for me this is at `C:\Users\Matt\jBPM\jbpm-jpdl-3.2.GA\server\server\jbpm\lib`.

Our `songs` database table contains the following columns:

- `ID`: an auto-incrementing field
- `song_name`: the name of the song that is input in the "Write songs" task
- `songwriter_name`: which we'll get from the username of whoever completes the "Write songs" task

We are going to achieve all this in jBPM through the use of **actions**. jBPM actions allow developers to execute bits of code when events are fired during the execution of the process. Actions can be represented as action nodes if it is relevant to see them in the process graph, or they can be hidden from the graph and executed behind the scenes. If they are put behind the scenes, they will normally be triggered by events such as the taking of a transition, entering a node or leaving a node.

For our purposes, we want our action to happen behind the scenes, as it isn't really relevant to the process actors we have using the system. We are going to place an action on the "leaving node" event of the "Write songs" task. This action will involve connecting to the `royalties` database and writing the process variables information to the database table.

Open up the Designer and browse through the Outline view to the "Write songs" task. Right-click on the node and select **Add Actions** then **Node Leave**:

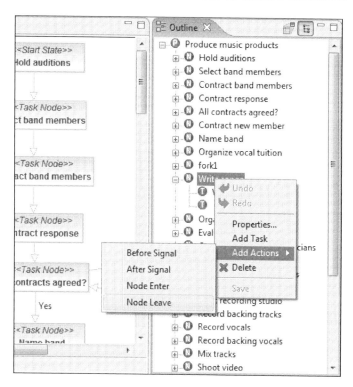

We will now see the new action attached to the event in the Outline view:

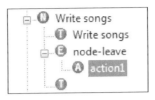

If we look at the Source view, we can see how this is translated into the raw XML:

```
<event type="node-leave">
    <action name="action1"></action>
</event>
```

Excellent, we now have an action that will be triggered every time the process goes through the "Write songs" task. It doesn't actually do anything yet though, as we still have to define exactly what we want the action to do. To do this, we need to add a new Java class to our project that will be the "action handler". Luckily, the jBPM folks have made this easy for us as they already include a sample action handler in the jBPM suite.

Expand the `src/main/java` element in the Package Explorer and you will find a package called `com.sample.action`: right-click this package and select **Copy**. Go back up to the `src/main/java` node of the tree, right-click and select **Paste**. Give your new package a name of `com.royaltiesadd.action`. Now expand out this new package and select the `MessageActionHandler.java` file within. In the **Refactor** menu at the top of the screen, select **Rename** and change the name to `RoyaltiesActionHandler.java`. The Designer is smart enough to change the internal naming of the Java class to our new naming convention. If we now double-click the `.java` file, we can see our new Java class:

Now, we need to replace the code in this Java class with the code that we need to extract the process variables and insert the data into the database. You can either type in the following code yourself or just use the file that's included in the download for this chapter. Don't worry too much about what's going on in the code, basically, we are just grabbing the song names from the process variables and the songwriter's name from the username of whoever is logged in, then inserting them into our database:

```
package com.royaltiesadd.action;

import org.jbpm.graph.def.ActionHandler;
import org.jbpm.graph.exe.ExecutionContext;
import java.sql.*;

public class RoyaltiesActionHandler implements ActionHandler {
    private static final long serialVersionUID = 1L;

    public void execute(ExecutionContext ctx) throws Exception {
        // get the fired employee from the process variables.
        String firstSong = (String) ctx.getContextInstance().getVariable("songName1");
        String secondSong = (String) ctx.getContextInstance().getVariable("songName2");
        String thirdSong = (String) ctx.getContextInstance().getVariable("songName3");
        String fourthSong = (String) ctx.getContextInstance().getVariable("songName4");
        String fifthSong = (String) ctx.getContextInstance().getVariable("songName5");
        String sixthSong = (String) ctx.getContextInstance().getVariable("songName6");
        String seventhSong = (String) ctx.getContextInstance().getVariable("songName7");
        String eighthSong = (String) ctx.getContextInstance().getVariable("songName8");
        String ninthSong = (String) ctx.getContextInstance().getVariable("songName9");
        String tenthSong = (String) ctx.getContextInstance().getVariable("songName10");
        String songWriterName = (String) ctx.getJbpmContext().getActorId();

        Connection con = null;
        try {
            Class.forName("com.mysql.jdbc.Driver").newInstance();
            con = DriverManager.getConnection("jdbc:mysql://localhost/royalties?user=root&password=secret");
            if (!con.isClosed())
```

```
                    //Now we add our data into the database
                    System.out.println("Connection successfully
established.");
                    Statement statement = con.createStatement();
                    statement.executeUpdate("INSERT INTO songs "
                        + "(ID,song_name,songwriter_name) "
                        + "VALUES (NULL,'" + firstSong + "','" +
songWriterName + "'),"
                        + "(NULL,'" + secondSong + "','" + songWriterName
+ "'),"
                        + "(NULL,'" + thirdSong + "','" + songWriterName
+ "'),"
                        + "(NULL,'" + fourthSong + "','" + songWriterName
+ "'),"
                        + "(NULL,'" + fifthSong + "','" + songWriterName
+ "'),"
                        + "(NULL,'" + sixthSong + "','" + songWriterName
+ "'),"
                        + "(NULL,'" + seventhSong + "','" +
songWriterName + "'),"
                        + "(NULL,'" + eighthSong + "','" + songWriterName
+ "'),"
                        + "(NULL,'" + ninthSong + "','" + songWriterName
+ "'),"
                        + "(NULL,'" + tenthSong + "','" + songWriterName
+ "')"
                    );
                    System.out.println("Songs and writers inserted.");
                    statement.close();
                    con.close();

            } catch(Exception e) {
                System.err.println("Exception: " + e.getMessage());
            } finally {
                try {
                    if(con != null)
                        con.close();
                } catch(SQLException e) {}
            }
        }
    }
```

Caveat: the above code is a simple demonstration of how to call out from jBPM, but you wouldn't want to tightly couple your process to a data store in this way in real life. In real life, it would be much better to use an action handler to access an external web service, which would itself perform domain model manipulation and sit on top of a persistence layer. That's far too complicated for a simple example like this though!

We now just need to tie together our new Java action handler class and the JPDL action. To do this, go back into the Outline view, right-click the **action1** action and select **Properties**. Switch to the **Handler** dialog and enter the full path and name of our action handler class `com.royaltiesadd.action.RoyaltiesActionHandler`:

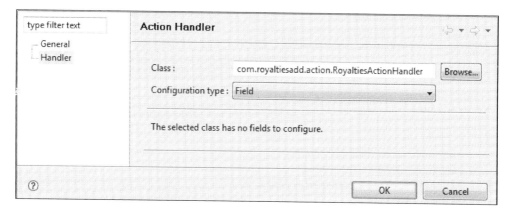

We deploy the process to the server, making sure we also check the `src/main/java` Java classes folder on the **Deployment** tab so our action handler is also deployed. Now, go through the process and get to the "Write songs" task form:

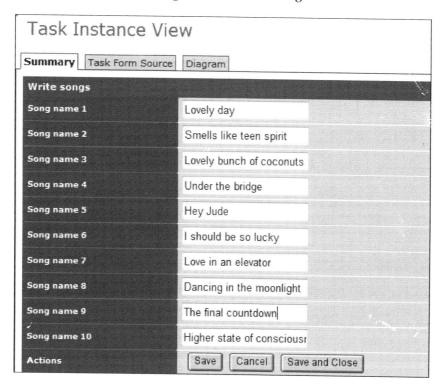

When we click the "Save and Close" button the process instance will leave the "Write songs" node, firing our action and causing our action handler Java class to run. If we now go into the database, we can see we have indeed managed to push the song and songwriter data into the database table:

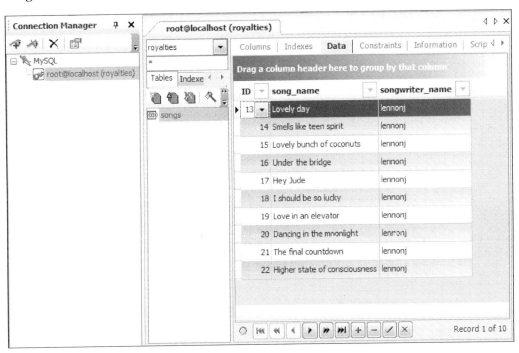

Clearly, as interfaces go, this is fairly hokum, but it is easy to appreciate how this simple example can be extended and built upon for a real-life application.

Obtain sign-off

After several iterations of testing and fixing periods, we should have got to a stage where all valid outstanding issues have been converted into a full scale change request because they are a scope change, closed down, fixed or are of such a low priority that we can proceed without a fix. We should make sure the change requests are properly documented, prioritized, and the work needed for the change is estimated.

Stepping back from the issues, is the original concept proved? Do our stakeholders buy into the system we've built? Is our sponsor on board and happy that this phase is complete? If the answer to these questions is yes, then we have achieved everything we wanted to from our proof of concept. Our system is fit for purpose and adequately supports the business process. We are now ready for full-scale UAT followed by go-live.

Summary

We've moved our system on leaps and bounds in this chapter and we're edging closer to having a system that is ready for live. We have put the jBPM system on a server, so our proof-of-concept testers can bash their test data into it and give us feedback on what they think. We have taken that feedback, sorted it into stuff that must be done now, and stuff that can be done later; and we've started making some of the changes we can do now.

We have allowed managers to prioritize tasks by design and on the fly. Most complicated of all, we have shown how our system can be integrated with other applications, both in house and external. We've done such a good job that our sponsor has happily signed off our proof-of-concept system.

We have now achieved our proof of concept and we're ready to move to full scale user acceptance testing and real implementation. This is what we'll do in the next chapter.

6
Proof-of-concept to implementation

With our proof-of-concept system maturing as a result of the iteration cycles we have taken it through, it is now time for us to start thinking about putting the system live. Before we do so, there are a number of tasks that we need to accomplish, as well as some optional changes we can make to improve the function of the system.

In this chapter, we'll look at how we judge when we are ready to start planning to go live and we'll cover the essentials we need to consider when building an implementation plan. We'll show how the web console can be customized according to your own branding and we'll see how we can swap the default jBPM database for a more robust, enterprise-ready database server. Finally, we'll look at the concept of business process monitoring and build our own process monitoring suite. The data collected by this suite will allow us to keep control over our process and to start to realize the return on investment that we promised our sponsors at the start of the project.

By the end of this chapter, we will have looked at the following deliverables:

- Implementation planning
- Web console customizations
- MySQL backend for jBPM
- Business process monitoring suite using the SeeWhy platform

Preparation for implementation

After taking our BPM system through several iterations, ironing out bugs, and smoothing the workflow as we go, at some point it will finally be time to put the thing live. Judging when we are ready for live is something of an art and it is important to prepare thoroughly for the big go-live date.

Judging readiness

So how do you know when your system is ready to go live? This is not an easy question to answer as every individual situation is different, and indeed you need to gaze into a crystal ball somewhat, as you don't necessarily want to wait until everything is 100% finished before you start the ramp-up for live. Generally speaking, when judging our readiness for live, we would at least want:

- To have the hardware the live system is going to run on in place.

- No critical change requests or issues outstanding. In most scenarios, it is probably OK to have development items on the change list: these can be implemented once the system is live.

- Confidence that there are no significant risks or issues that will stop us obtaining sign-off from our sponsor that we are ready for live.

If the above criteria are met then it is time for us to develop a detailed implementation plan and to start gearing ourselves up for go-live.

Implementation plan

Going live with a business process critical system such as this should not be taken lightly. A proper implementation plan is essential, even if there is always the possibility that the business process could just continue on in the current state if something happens to the new system. Unfortunately, every business situation will be different, so it is practically impossible to provide a template implementation plan where you simply fill out the blanks. Nevertheless, the following table sets out a checklist of things to consider when putting together an implementation plan.

Area of consideration	Detail	Notes
IT	Hardware	Hardware tests, performance tests, redundancy, failover, and backup planning. Security.
	Hardware and network support	Who will support the hardware and network? When should they be available to us during the go-live period? Service level agreements.

Area of consideration	Detail	Notes
BPM application	Non-BPM software support (browsers, operating systems, and so on)	Support for the systems we are integrating with. Cutover resources. Warn helpdesk about our implementation. Do helpdesk require support scripts? Service level agreements.
	System administration	Who will administer the system? Dedicated resource or part-time? What is expected of them? Service level agreement? User set up.
	Super users	First line of support? What is expected of them? What is the incentive to be a super user?
	Installation	Who is responsible? When do we need them during the go-live period? Hand over to business as usual support.
	Monitoring	Who will monitor the system once it is live? What do we expect them to do if there are problems? What is the escalation path? Change request process post-go-live.
Cutover	Go-live date and timelines	Set a realistic target date, working backwards with all tasks that need to be accomplished.
	How will we go live?	Parallel running or "big bang"?
	Contingency	Plan for the worst case scenario.
	Global implications	If implementing globally, which time zone should go live first? Any language implications for the plan?
	Intense support	Set up a "war room": special phone lines and email addresses. 24x7 availability of critical people.
Communications	User community	Make sure all our end users are aware of our implementation date and what is expected of them. "Show and tell" sessions led by the users involved in the proof-of-concept?
	Other stakeholders	Indirectly affected by the implementation: suppliers, customers other departments. Review our stakeholder analysis.
Training	User training	When and where? Who will do the training? "Just in time" training is best.

Customizing the web console

Some business process management suites offer complete solutions for building a highly customized graphical user interface to your process definition. For instance, the Singularity Process Platform has a "drag and drop" development environment that the process developer uses to customize the front end web files that the platform generates. JBoss jBPM isn't this advanced yet, and if we want to make changes to the default web console pages, we have to either limit ourselves to editing the XHTML task forms or throw the whole lot away and build our own. Building your own web console or Windows application front end to the process engine is entirely possible and probably advisable in large-scale implementations. The web console and sample enterprise application that come with the jBPM suite download can act as reference material for your own designs.

For our purposes, just before we go live, we probably want to do some minor customization to the web console. For example, we may want to replace the JBoss logo with our own company or department logo, change the colors, font, and so on. You may also want to add a few more links into the navigation side bar: to your process documentation or support website for example. Fortunately, this is relatively easy to accomplish and we'll go through the steps here. For more advanced customization, it is best to leave the work to a professional Java developer, but we can make simple changes ourselves.

Furthermore, it is worth bearing in mind that making wide-ranging customizations to the web console may well mean that upgrading to newer versions that are released by the JBoss jBPM project is made that much more difficult. Also, getting access to upgrades released by the project community is one of the principle benefits of using an open-source product, so it is worthwhile trying to work with as vanilla a version as possible.

Nevertheless, it should be relatively easy to retrofit the simplistic amendments that we'll do here into future versions of the web console. First off, we need to get the source code for the web console. Luckily, the project team have kindly given us a copy of the code with our jBPM installation. Look in the `deploy` directory at the top level of your jBPM installation: you should see a file called `jbpm-console.war` in there. For me, this is at `C:\Users\Matt\jBPM\jbpm-jpdl-3.2.GA\deploy`. This `.war` file is simply a compressed version of a regular folder structure, much like a ZIP file. In fact, we can open this file with a regular ZIP file utility and inspect its contents. On my machine, I have a ZIP utility called 7-Zip, though any ZIP tool should do the job. Open the `.war` file and extract it to a handy location: a folder on your desktop for example. When extracted, the directory structure should be clearly visible, like this:

Name	Date modified	Type	Size
common	31/03/2007 18:19	File Folder	
css	31/03/2007 18:19	File Folder	
images	31/03/2007 18:19	File Folder	
js	31/03/2007 18:19	File Folder	
main	31/03/2007 18:19	File Folder	
META-INF	31/03/2007 18:19	File Folder	
search	31/03/2007 18:19	File Folder	
WEB-INF	31/03/2007 18:19	File Folder	
index.jsp	25/01/2007 13:59	JSP File	1 KB

We don't need to worry about most of these folders and, in fact, we should be careful not to edit or delete any by mistake because it may cause the web console to stop working. We need to focus on the `css` and `images` folders to make cosmetic changes to the web console. Go into the `images` folder and find the `background.gif` file. Make a backup copy of this image and then open up the original in your favorite image editor: I use the GIMP. Make any changes that you want to the logo and save the file. I have blanked out the "JBoss" logo in the top left corner and replaced it with my own "Bland Records" logo. You could change the colours or do whatever you want:

Now that we've made our changes, we need to save our folder structure back to a `.war` file. To do this, we will use a built in Java command-line utility called "jar". This just makes sure that the `.war` file is built in the correct way. Open up a command line (**Start | Run** | type "cmd"). Use the CD command to change directory to the folder where you extracted the web console code: make sure you are at the top level of that folder structure. The command will be something like:

```
CD C:\Users\Matt\Desktop\jbpm-console\
```

Now we need to run the `jar` utility with the following command; make sure to type it exactly as it appears below:

```
jar cMf jbpm-console.war *
```

After a moment's thinking about it, the `jar` utility should do its job and create a file called `jbpm-console.war` in the top level of our temporary folder:

Name	Date modified	Type	Size
common	31/03/2007 18:19	File Folder	
css	31/03/2007 18:19	File Folder	
images	31/03/2007 18:19	File Folder	
js	31/03/2007 18:19	File Folder	
main	31/03/2007 18:19	File Folder	
META-INF	31/03/2007 18:19	File Folder	
search	31/03/2007 18:19	File Folder	
WEB-INF	31/03/2007 18:19	File Folder	
index.jsp	25/01/2007 13:59	JSP File	1 KB
jbpm-console.war	01/04/2007 09:39	WAR File	4,631 KB

Now we need to deploy this amended web console to our application server. Go to the `deploy` folder of the JBoss application server installation (note that this is not the `deploy` folder at the top level of the installation). For me, this is at `C:\Users\Matt\jBPM\jbpm-jpdl-3.2.GA\server\server\jbpm\deploy`. In this folder, you will see that there is already a `jbpm-console.war` in there: this is the currently deployed web console. Move this file to a safe location in a different folder, so we can bring it back in if we've made a mistake. Now copy our newly-created `jbpm-console.war` into the `deploy` folder. Start up the JBoss application server and browse to the web console. After logging in, you should see that the changes we have made have taken effect:

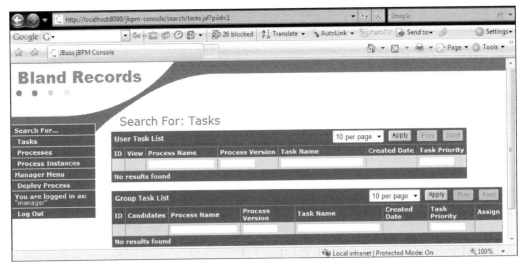

Obviously, this is a simple example, but you can clearly see how this could be extended to make other changes to the web console.

Swapping the database back end

The Hypersonic database that comes with jBPM is an excellent database for developing and prototyping an application, but it doesn't have the level of robustness that we need for our live application. Further, we are going to want to mine the data that our application produces, and this will be much easier to do if the database back end is a full-scale enterprise database.

JBoss jBPM supports a number of enterprise databases, including the ubiquitous Oracle, DB2 and Microsoft SQL Server. Which database you choose is most likely to be influenced by whatever flavor of enterprise database you use in the rest of your organization. We will swap the Hypersonic database for MySQL because it is freely available, highly stable, and easy to install. Let's go through the steps for swapping out the back end on a Windows machine.

Install the database server

Go to `http://dev.mysql.com/downloads/mysql/4.1.html` and download the relevant version of MySQL for your operating system; in our case this is Windows. Ensure you download version 4.1 as version 5 has been known to cause a few problems with JBoss jBPM. Once downloaded, install the database on your server machine, accepting the defaults given to you by the installation program.

Now that MySQL is installed, start the server (this is in the **Services** dialog of **Administrative Tools** in the **Control Panel** on Windows). Go to **Program Files | MySQL | MySQL Server 4.1 | MySQL Command Line Client**. You should be presented with a dialog similar to the following:

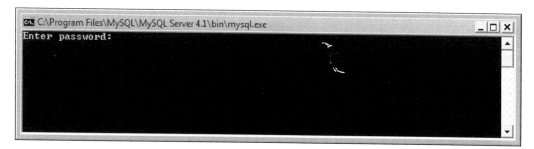

Enter the password that you gave during the installation routine and you will be granted access to the database server. Now, we need to create our database and to do this we need to type in some simple SQL. Type in the following line, taking care to type it exactly:

```
CREATE DATABASE IF NOT EXISTS jbpmbackend;
```

Note the semicolon at the end of the line. If all goes well MySQL should confirm that the database has been created:

```
C:\Program Files\MySQL\MySQL Server 4.1\bin\mysql.exe
Enter password: *******
Welcome to the MySQL monitor.  Commands end with ; or \g.
Your MySQL connection id is 3 to server version: 4.1.22-community-nt

Type 'help;' or '\h' for help. Type '\c' to clear the buffer.

mysql> CREATE DATABASE IF NOT EXISTS jbpmbackend;
Query OK, 1 row affected (0.20 sec)

mysql>
```

Install the database tables

Now that we have our database ready to go, we have to set up the database tables that jBPM will use to hold its data. The JBoss jBPM project has provided us with a head start on this by creating a ready-made SQL script that we can use to set up the database schema we need. Unfortunately, this script does need a bit of amendment before we can run it, but we'll see the steps to make it ready.

If you look in the db folder of your jBPM installation, you will see a number of .sql files (for me this is at C:\Users\Matt\jBPM\jbpm-jpdl-3.2.GA\db). You will notice that there is one of these .sql files for most of the popular enterprise databases, including Oracle, IBM DB2, and Microsoft SQL Server. Of course, we want the one for MySQL and this is called jbpm.jpdl.mysql.sql. To run this SQL script on our server, we first need to make sure that we run the script against our new database. Type the following exactly in the command-line client:

```
USE jbpmbackend
```

We then need to tell the server to run our script, but as mentioned above, unfortunately the default jbpm.jpdl.mysql.sql script doesn't work out of the box. We need to make some alterations to it. Open up the file in a text editor and delete the following lines from the start of the script:

```
alter table JBPM_ACTION drop foreign key FK_ACTION_EVENT
alter table JBPM_ACTION drop foreign key FK_ACTION_EXPTHDL
alter table JBPM_ACTION drop foreign key FK_ACTION_PROCDEF
alter table JBPM_ACTION drop foreign key FK_CRTETIMERACT_TA
alter table JBPM_ACTION drop foreign key FK_ACTION_ACTNDEL
alter table JBPM_ACTION drop foreign key FK_ACTION_REFACT
alter table JBPM_BYTEARRAY drop foreign key FK_BYTEARR_FILDEF
alter table JBPM_BYTEBLOCK drop foreign key FK_BYTEBLOCK_FILE
alter table JBPM_COMMENT drop foreign key FK_COMMENT_TOKEN
alter table JBPM_COMMENT drop foreign key FK_COMMENT_TSK
alter table JBPM_DECISIONCONDITIONS drop foreign key FK_DECCOND_DEC
```

```
alter table JBPM_DELEGATION drop foreign key FK_DELEGATION_PRCD
alter table JBPM_EVENT drop foreign key FK_EVENT_PROCDEF
alter table JBPM_EVENT drop foreign key FK_EVENT_NODE
alter table JBPM_EVENT drop foreign key FK_EVENT_TRANS
alter table JBPM_EVENT drop foreign key FK_EVENT_TASK
alter table JBPM_JOB drop foreign key FK_JOB_TOKEN
alter table JBPM_JOB drop foreign key FK_JOB_NODE
alter table JBPM_JOB drop foreign key FK_JOB_PRINST
alter table JBPM_JOB drop foreign key FK_JOB_ACTION
alter table JBPM_JOB drop foreign key FK_JOB_TSKINST
alter table JBPM_LOG drop foreign key FK_LOG_SOURCENODE
alter table JBPM_LOG drop foreign key FK_LOG_TOKEN
alter table JBPM_LOG drop foreign key FK_LOG_OLDBYTES
alter table JBPM_LOG drop foreign key FK_LOG_NEWBYTES
alter table JBPM_LOG drop foreign key FK_LOG_CHILDTOKEN
alter table JBPM_LOG drop foreign key FK_LOG_DESTNODE
alter table JBPM_LOG drop foreign key FK_LOG_TASKINST
alter table JBPM_LOG drop foreign key FK_LOG_SWIMINST
alter table JBPM_LOG drop foreign key FK_LOG_PARENT
alter table JBPM_LOG drop foreign key FK_LOG_NODE
alter table JBPM_LOG drop foreign key FK_LOG_ACTION
alter table JBPM_LOG drop foreign key FK_LOG_VARINST
alter table JBPM_LOG drop foreign key FK_LOG_TRANSITION
alter table JBPM_MODULEDEFINITION drop foreign key FK_TSKDEF_START
alter table JBPM_MODULEDEFINITION drop foreign key FK_MODDEF_PROCDEF
alter table JBPM_MODULEINSTANCE drop foreign key FK_TASKMGTINST_TMD
alter table JBPM_MODULEINSTANCE drop foreign key FK_MODINST_PRCINST
alter table JBPM_NODE drop foreign key FK_PROCST_SBPRCDEF
alter table JBPM_NODE drop foreign key FK_NODE_PROCDEF
alter table JBPM_NODE drop foreign key FK_NODE_SCRIPT
alter table JBPM_NODE drop foreign key FK_NODE_ACTION
alter table JBPM_NODE drop foreign key FK_DECISION_DELEG
alter table JBPM_NODE drop foreign key FK_NODE_SUPERSTATE
alter table JBPM_POOLEDACTOR drop foreign key FK_POOLEDACTOR_SLI
alter table JBPM_PROCESSDEFINITION drop foreign key FK_PROCDEF_STRTSTA
alter table JBPM_PROCESSINSTANCE drop foreign key FK_PROCIN_PROCDEF
alter table JBPM_PROCESSINSTANCE drop foreign key FK_PROCIN_ROOTTKN
alter table JBPM_PROCESSINSTANCE drop foreign key FK_PROCIN_SPROCTKN
alter table JBPM_RUNTIMEACTION drop foreign key FK_RTACTN_PROCINST
alter table JBPM_RUNTIMEACTION drop foreign key FK_RTACTN_ACTION
alter table JBPM_SWIMLANE drop foreign key FK_SWL_ASSDEL
alter table JBPM_SWIMLANE drop foreign key FK_SWL_TSKMGMTDEF
alter table JBPM_SWIMLANEINSTANCE drop foreign key FK_SWIMLANEINST_TM
alter table JBPM_SWIMLANEINSTANCE drop foreign key FK_SWIMLANEINST_SL
alter table JBPM_TASK drop foreign key FK_TSK_TSKCTRL
alter table JBPM_TASK drop foreign key FK_TASK_ASSDEL
alter table JBPM_TASK drop foreign key FK_TASK_TASKNODE
```

```
alter table JBPM_TASK drop foreign key FK_TASK_PROCDEF
alter table JBPM_TASK drop foreign key FK_TASK_STARTST
alter table JBPM_TASK drop foreign key FK_TASK_TASKMGTDEF
alter table JBPM_TASK drop foreign key FK_TASK_SWIMLANE
alter table JBPM_TASKACTORPOOL drop foreign key FK_TSKACTPOL_PLACT
alter table JBPM_TASKACTORPOOL drop foreign key FK_TASKACTPL_TSKI
alter table JBPM_TASKCONTROLLER drop foreign key FK_TSKCTRL_DELEG
alter table JBPM_TASKINSTANCE drop foreign key FK_TSKINS_PRCINS
alter table JBPM_TASKINSTANCE drop foreign key FK_TASKINST_TMINST
alter table JBPM_TASKINSTANCE drop foreign key FK_TASKINST_TOKEN
alter table JBPM_TASKINSTANCE drop foreign key FK_TASKINST_SLINST
alter table JBPM_TASKINSTANCE drop foreign key FK_TASKINST_TASK
alter table JBPM_TOKEN drop foreign key FK_TOKEN_PARENT
alter table JBPM_TOKEN drop foreign key FK_TOKEN_NODE
alter table JBPM_TOKEN drop foreign key FK_TOKEN_PROCINST
alter table JBPM_TOKEN drop foreign key FK_TOKEN_SUBPI
alter table JBPM_TOKENVARIABLEMAP drop foreign key FK_TKVARMAP_CTXT
alter table JBPM_TOKENVARIABLEMAP drop foreign key FK_TKVARMAP_TOKEN
alter table JBPM_TRANSITION drop foreign key FK_TRANSITION_TO
alter table JBPM_TRANSITION drop foreign key FK_TRANS_PROCDEF
alter table JBPM_TRANSITION drop foreign key FK_TRANSITION_FROM
alter table JBPM_VARIABLEACCESS drop foreign key FK_VARACC_TSKCTRL
alter table JBPM_VARIABLEACCESS drop foreign key FK_VARACC_SCRIPT
alter table JBPM_VARIABLEACCESS drop foreign key FK_VARACC_PROCST
alter table JBPM_VARIABLEINSTANCE drop foreign key FK_VARINST_TK
alter table JBPM_VARIABLEINSTANCE drop foreign key FK_VARINST_TKVARMP
alter table JBPM_VARIABLEINSTANCE drop foreign key FK_VARINST_PRCINST
alter table JBPM_VARIABLEINSTANCE drop foreign key FK_VAR_TSKINST
alter table JBPM_VARIABLEINSTANCE drop foreign key FK_BYTEINST_ARRAY
```

We then need to type a semicolon at the end of every line in the file: a tedious but necessary job as MySQL demands this syntax. Finally, the default script doesn't include the tables that are needed to control access in the web console. To do this, we need to add the following lines of SQL code to the end of the file:

```
CREATE TABLE JBPM_ID_GROUP(ID_ BIGINT NOT NULL auto_increment,CLASS_
CHAR(1) NOT NULL,NAME_ VARCHAR(255),TYPE_ VARCHAR(255),PARENT_
BIGINT,primary key(ID_)) type=InnoDB;

alter table JBPM_ID_GROUP add index FK_ID_GRP_PARENT (PARENT_),add
constraint FK_ID_GRP_PARENT foreign key (PARENT_) references JBPM_ID_
GROUP(ID_);

CREATE  TABLE JBPM_ID_MEMBERSHIP(ID_ BIGINT NOT NULL auto_
increment,CLASS_ CHAR(1) NOT NULL,NAME_ VARCHAR(255),ROLE_
VARCHAR(255),USER_ BIGINT,GROUP_ BIGINT,primary key(ID_)) type=InnoDB;
alter table JBPM_ID_MEMBERSHIP add index FK_ID_MEMSHIP_GRP (GROUP_
),add constraint FK_ID_MEMSHIP_GRP foreign key (GROUP_) references
JBPM_ID_GROUP(ID_);
```

```
CREATE TABLE JBPM_ID_PERMISSIONS(ENTITY_ BIGINT NOT NULL,CLASS_
VARCHAR(255),NAME_ VARCHAR(255),ACTION_ VARCHAR(255)) type=InnoDB;

CREATE  TABLE JBPM_ID_USER(ID_ BIGINT NOT NULL auto_increment,CLASS_
CHAR(1) NOT NULL,NAME_ VARCHAR(255),EMAIL_ VARCHAR(255),PASSWORD_
VARCHAR(255),primary key(ID_)) type=InnoDB;

ALTER TABLE JBPM_ID_MEMBERSHIP ADD index FK_ID_MEMSHIP_USR (USER_),add
CONSTRAINT FK_ID_MEMSHIP_USR FOREIGN KEY(USER_) REFERENCES JBPM_ID_
USER(ID_);

INSERT INTO JBPM_ID_GROUP VALUES(1,'G','sales','organisation',NULL);
INSERT INTO JBPM_ID_GROUP VALUES(2,'G','hr','organisation',NULL);
INSERT INTO JBPM_ID_GROUP VALUES(3,'G','participant','security-
role',NULL);
INSERT INTO JBPM_ID_GROUP VALUES(4,'G','manager','security-
role',NULL);
INSERT INTO JBPM_ID_GROUP VALUES(5,'G','administrator','security-
role',NULL);
INSERT INTO JBPM_ID_USER VALUES(1,'U','cookie monster','cookie.
monster@sesamestreet.tv','cookie monster');
INSERT INTO JBPM_ID_USER VALUES(2,'U','ernie','ernie@sesamestreet.
tv','ernie');
INSERT INTO JBPM_ID_USER VALUES(3,'U','bert','bert@sesamestreet.
tv','bert');
INSERT INTO JBPM_ID_USER VALUES(4,'U','grover','grover@sesamestreet.
tv','grover');
INSERT INTO JBPM_ID_MEMBERSHIP VALUES(1,'M',NULL,NULL,1,3);
INSERT INTO JBPM_ID_MEMBERSHIP VALUES(2,'M',NULL,NULL,2,3);
INSERT INTO JBPM_ID_MEMBERSHIP VALUES(3,'M',NULL,NULL,4,2);
INSERT INTO JBPM_ID_MEMBERSHIP VALUES(4,'M',NULL,NULL,4,3);
INSERT INTO JBPM_ID_MEMBERSHIP VALUES(5,'M',NULL,NULL,3,3);
INSERT INTO JBPM_ID_MEMBERSHIP VALUES(6,'M',NULL,NULL,3,2);
INSERT INTO JBPM_ID_MEMBERSHIP VALUES(7,'M',NULL,NULL,2,2);
INSERT INTO JBPM_ID_MEMBERSHIP VALUES(8,'M',NULL,NULL,2,4);
INSERT INTO JBPM_ID_MEMBERSHIP VALUES(9,'M',NULL,NULL,2,5);
INSERT INTO JBPM_ID_MEMBERSHIP VALUES(10,'M',NULL,'boss',2,1);
INSERT INTO JBPM_ID_MEMBERSHIP VALUES(11,'M',NULL,NULL,1,1);
```

There is a pre-altered version of this script in the download for this chapter if you don't feel like straining your typing finger. With the file altered, save it and go back to the MySQL command line. Type in:

```
source path_to_your_jbpm.jpdl.mysql.sql_file
```

If all goes well then we should be rewarded with a long list of "Query OK" confirmations from MySQL. Our database tables are now all set up and ready to receive the data needed to run the web console.

Import the data

With our database tables set up, we must now set up our users. This is simply a matter of running a MySQL-ized version of the SQL scripts we used in Chapter 4. There is a file included in the download for this chapter called `insert-user-info-mysql.sql`, and this is what we should use to set up our users. Assuming that your user group is going to expand for go-live, you should edit this file to include details of every user who will need access to the live system. Once the file is ready, in the MySQL command-line client, type:

```
source path_to_inser-user-info-mysql_file
```

When you have run all the scripts, you can check to see if the users are set up by entering:

```
SELECT * FROM JBPM_ID_USER;
```

All being well, the command-line client should confirm back that the user table contains the details of all our users:

Set up a JNDI data source

With our database set up and ready to go, we must now tell JBoss to use this database rather than the Hypersonic one it uses by default. The first step is to set up what's called a "JNDI data source". This is a simple XML file that tells the JBoss server where to find the database, and the connection details it needs to get access. Move the `jbpm-ds.xml` file (you can find in the `deploy` directory of your JBoss server installation) to a safe location for backup: for me this file is at `C:\Users\Matt\jBPM\jbpm-jpdl-3.2.GA\server\server\jbpm\deploy`. With the old data source file safely backed up, create a new file called `jbpm-ds.xml` in the `deploy` directory and type the following XML code into it:

```xml
<?xml version="1.0" encoding="UTF-8"?>

<datasources>
  <local-tx-datasource>
    <jndi-name>JbpmDS</jndi-name>
    <connection-url>jdbc:mysql://localhost:3306/jbpmbackend</connection-url>
    <driver-class>com.mysql.jdbc.Driver</driver-class>
    <user-name>root</user-name>
    <password>secret</password>
    <metadata>
      <type-mapping>MySQL</type-mapping>
    </metadata>
  </local-tx-datasource>
</datasources>
```

Remember to change the database server URL, user name, and password information that are highlighted above to suit what you specified during the installation of MySQL. Again, there is a copy of this `jbpm-ds.xml` file in the download for this chapter.

Install the MySQL driver

We must also provide the JBoss server with the driver it needs to connect to MySQL. Download the MySQL Connector/J package from `http://www.mysql.com/downloads/api-jdbc.html`. Extract the ZIP file that you have downloaded and put the resulting `.jar` file into the `lib` folder of your JBoss server installation: for me, this is at `C:\Users\Matt\jBPM\jbpm-jpdl-3.2.GA\server\server\jbpm\lib`.

Amend the JBoss configuration

The JBoss application server uses several other configuration files to manage its connection to a database, and we need to make sure those files are amended to point to our new MySQL database.

Find the `login-config.xml` file in the `conf` directory of the JBoss server installation:
for me this is at `C:\Users\Matt\jBPM\jbpm-jpdl-3.2.GA\server\server\jbpm\`
`conf`. Make a backup of this file, and then open it up so we can amend it. Add the
following code to the end of the file:

```
<application-policy name = "jbpm">
  <authentication>
      <login-module code="org.jboss.security.auth.spi.
DatabaseServerLoginModule" flag="required">
         <module-option name="dsJndiName">java:/JbpmDS</module-
option>
         <module-option name="principalsQuery">
           SELECT PASSWORD_ FROM JBPM_ID_USER WHERE NAME_=?
         </module-option>
         <module-option name="rolesQuery">
           SELECT g.NAME_ ,'Roles'
           FROM JBPM_ID_USER u,
               JBPM_ID_MEMBERSHIP m,
               JBPM_ID_GROUP g
           WHERE g.TYPE_='security-role'
             AND m.GROUP_ = g.ID_
             AND m.USER_ = u.ID_
             AND u.NAME_=?
         </module-option>
      </login-module>
   </authentication>
</application-policy>
```

Next, we need to amend the `standardjaws.xml` file that is also in the `conf` directory.
Make a back up of it, then open up the file and find the `<datasource>` element at the
top of the file. Replace the `<datasource>` and `<type-mapping>` elements with the
code highlighted below:

```
<jaws>
    <datasource>java:/JbpmDS</datasource>
    <type-mapping>mySQL</type-mapping>
    <debug>false</debug>

    <default-entity>
       <create-table>true</create-table>
       <remove-table>false</remove-table>
       <tuned-updates>true</tuned-updates>
       <read-only>false</read-only>
       <time-out>300</time-out>
       <row-locking>false</row-locking>
       <read-ahead>false</read-ahead>
    </default-entity>
```

Amend the hibernate configuration

Almost there! Finally, we need to amend the Hibernate configuration that jBPM uses to manage the persistence of its Java objects to the database. Basically, this means telling jBPM to save its data to MySQL rather than the old Hypersonic database.

The first step is to change the Hibernate configuration in our web console. As we did above, this involves editing the source code for the web console. Go back into the extracted source code and navigate to the `WEB-INF\classes` directory. Open up the `hibernate.cfg.xml` file that is located there. Amend the code in the file with the lines highlighted below, taking care to use the URL, username, and password for your MySQL configuration:

```
<?xml version='1.0' encoding='utf-8'?>

<!DOCTYPE hibernate-configuration PUBLIC
        "-//Hibernate/Hibernate Configuration DTD 3.0//EN"
        "http://hibernate.sourceforge.net/hibernate-configuration-
3.0.dtd">

<hibernate-configuration>
  <session-factory>

    <!-- hibernate dialect -->
    <!--<property name="hibernate.dialect">org.hibernate.dialect.
HSQLDialect</property> -->
    <property name="hibernate.dialect">org.hibernate.dialect.
MySQLDialect</property>

    <!-- JDBC connection properties (begin) -->
    <property name="hibernate.connection.driver_class">com.mysql.jdbc.
Driver</property>
    <property name="hibernate.connection.url">jdbc:mysql://
localhost:3306/jbpmbackend</property>
    <property name="hibernate.connection.username">root</property>
    <property name="hibernate.connection.password">secret</property>
    <!-- JDBC connection properties (end) -->
        <property name="hibernate.cache.provider_class">org.hibernate.
cache.HashtableCacheProvider</property>

    <!-- DataSource properties (begin) -->
    <property name="hibernate.connection.datasource">java:/JbpmDS</
property>
    <!-- DataSource properties (end) -->

    <!-- JTA transaction properties (begin)  === 
    <property name="hibernate.transaction.factory_class">org.
hibernate.transaction.JTATransactionFactory</property>
```

```
    <property name="hibernate.transaction.manager_lookup_class">org.
hibernate.transaction.JBossTransactionManagerLookup</property>
    <property name="jta.UserTransaction">/UserTransaction</property>

    ==== JTA transaction properties (end) -->
.....
```

We've abbreviated the code for convenience: you can find a copy of the amended file in the download for this chapter. Now we need to use our Jar utility to make a new `jbpm-console.war` file to deploy. As before, open up a command line, change to the top level of the directory with the web console code in it, and run the following command:

```
jar cMf jbpm-console.war *
```

Paste the newly created `jbpm-console.war` file into the deploy directory of the server: for me, this is at `C:\Users\Matt\jBPM\jbpm-jpdl-3.2.GA\server\server\jbpm\deploy`. Our web console is now configured to use the new database. If we now start up the application server and browse to the web console, we can see that the slate has been wiped clean and we now have version 1 of our process definition deployed in jBPM and running on MySQL:

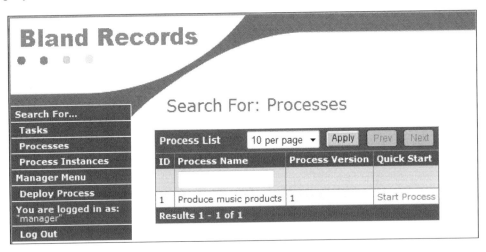

Monitoring the process

Business Activity Monitoring, or "BAM", is a buzzword that is bandied around a lot by consultants and management, but unfortunately, it is generally poorly understood. Usually, this results in business process management projects being told to, "do some BAM", but this vague instruction is open to interpretation and often leads to poorly-thought out implementations that don't provide anything valuable.

So, before we dive in and, "do some BAM", we'd better understand exactly what we are talking about. In reality, there are three different sides to process monitoring:

- Process management
- Process metrics analysis
- Process forecasting

You'll notice that none of these actually include "Business Activity Monitoring". I have deliberately shied away from this catch-all terminology in order to work with a tighter definition of what we actually want to achieve by monitoring our process. The combination of these three elements will encompass everything that is usually meant by "business activity monitoring". Each of these three elements must be mastered if the BPM implementation is to be successful. Let's look at a definition of each process monitoring element.

Process management

Process management is about monitoring individual instances of the process as they are executed. It is an activity that happens in real time, allowing management to stay abreast of operations and keep track of time overruns, delays, and bottlenecks as they occur. This is a vital tool for managing the process on a day-to-day level. For example, if a particular task is meant to take three hours to complete, but a particular process instance has been stuck on the task for six hours, the system can notify management of the delay, allowing them to take corrective action.

Process metrics analysis

Process metrics analysis is a backward-looking activity that analyzes trends in aggregated historical process instance data. This is an activity that has been part a of business process work since before business process management systems were available. Previously, process metrics were analyzed based on data that were estimated by the analyst and the users, but now that we are able to capture the exact data in the BPM system, we can draw conclusions from a much more accurate data set. For example, we will now have exact data for the average time it takes to complete a certain task node. We can analyze the trends in this average to see if the process is running more or less efficiently, helping us to identify and deal with bottlenecks. Typically, we are going to want to track metrics like "average time per task per actor" or "average throughput per month".

Process forecasting

The final element of our process monitoring solution is forecasting the date on which we expect process instances to complete. We should be able to forecast this date for individual instances, as well as aggregating all instances that are executing: we can use these forecasts to plan the company's pipeline. For example, in the case of Bland Records, we will want to know how many albums are expected to release in March 2008, allowing us to smooth the pipeline over several months, if it would be beneficial.

Example process reporting suite

JBoss has recently announced a partnership with SeeWhy that is intended to provide many of the business activity monitoring capabilities that are missing from the jBPM suite at the moment. SeeWhy produces a business intelligence platform that also runs on the JBoss application server and which we can integrate with jBPM. We will use SeeWhy to provide our "process management" reporting and notification solution. It should be noted that jBPM does provide some notification functionality, but as SeeWhy is much more flexible, we have decided to use it instead. The most powerful aspect of SeeWhy is its real-time analysis of incoming process data: if we expect an operation to take three hours then SeeWhy can tell us as soon as it takes longer than three hours. This being said, we will also use the SeeWhy platform for the, "process metrics analysis", and, "process forecasting", elements of our reporting suite. We could use any data mining and report presentation technology for these elements, but as we'll already have SeeWhy set up, we have decided to go with that. If we really wanted to keep things simple, we could simply export the data from our MySQL database as an Excel spreadsheet and mess around with it by hand, but it is nice to see how this can be automated with the SeeWhy toolset.

Integrating the SeeWhy business intelligence platform

The SeeWhy Business Intelligence platform is designed to accept "event" data from other systems and transform that raw data into useful information. This useful information can then drive management notifications and dashboard reports. When put together with jBPM, the combined software architecture looks something like this:

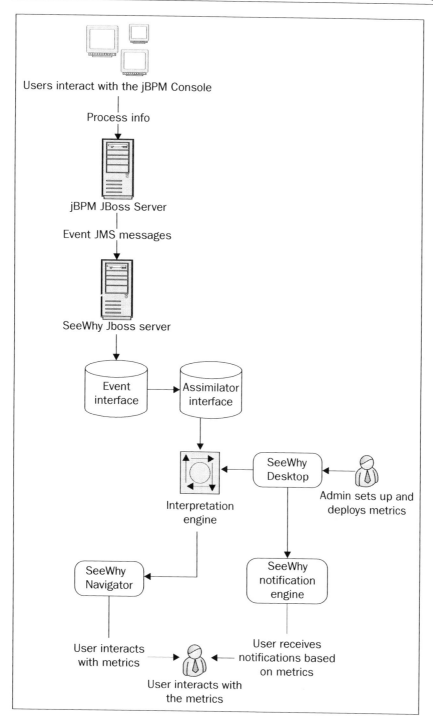

External systems send messages into the SeeWhy Event Interface. This then passes the messages on to the Assimilator, which ensures that the event data is safely stored. The data is then passed on to the Interpretation Engine, which runs the business rules and calculations for the appropriate metric that have been configured in the SeeWhy Desktop. The Presentation layer then formats the metrics and presents the data through the SeeWhy Navigator. The Notification layer sends out notifications to end users based on a comparison between metric rules that have been set up and the data that is coming through. Let's set it up and see what we can do with it.

Get SeeWhy

First of all, we need to get the software installed onto the machine that we are going to use. We are going to mimic a typical production environment and install SeeWhy on a separate machine from the server that we are using for jBPM. As a pre-requisite, we will need to have version 5 of MySQL installed on the server machine that we are going to use. Go to `http://www.seewhy.com` and register with the website. Once you have completed the registration procedure and are signed in, locate the download page at `http://www.seewhy.com/download` and download the SeeWhy community edition of the software for your operating system. We will use the Windows version that includes the Java VM: if you already have Java installed then select the version without Java VM.

Install SeeWhy

Unzip the file you have downloaded to a convenient location and double-click the `.exe` file to start the installer. The first step is to choose a Java VM for SeeWhy to use. If you are using the version of the installer that comes with a Java VM then just use that, otherwise, you'll have to search your machine for it yourself. Mine is located at `C:\Program Files\Java\jdk1.5.0_11\bin\java.exe`. Choose "No" when the installer asks you if you have an existing JBoss instance you wish to use. Accept the default folder that the installer gives you for the JBoss installation; the installer will then download JBoss and install it to the specified location.

With JBoss installed, we must now connect SeeWhy to our MySQL database. When prompted, select a database type of MySQL. Next, select, "**I want to use a local database server**", then, "**Yes, I have an existing MySQL instance I want to use**". Select, "**I will choose a MySQL folder**", then browse to your MySQL installation folder; for me, this is at `C:\Program Files\MySQL\MySQL Server 5.0`.

We must then install the database connector that will allow JBoss to connect to MySQL. Select, "**I want to download a database connector**", and the installer will download the necessary from the MySQL website.

When prompted, enter the details of your MySQL installation, making sure MySQL is running so that SeeWhy can connect to it. If your version of MySQL is less than 5.0.27 then you will probably get a warning telling you that you are using the wrong version. Don't worry about this; ignore the warning and continue the installation.

Enter a SeeWhy container name of "seewhy". Next, click "**Yes, install an email server for me**". Accept the default installation directory that the installer gives you. After this, accept the default location for the SeeWhy installation files and finally click **Install**.

Once the installation routine has run, we need to perform a few configuration steps to complete the installation. Call the database `seewhy` and accept the other defaults. Again you may get a warning that it is the wrong database: ignore this warning and continue. All being well, SeeWhy should now be installed and be operational. To test the installation, go to the `C:\SeeWhy Community Edition V3.2\SeeWhy_Tutorial\` folder and double-click the `Start SeeWhy Server.bat` file. Once the start up routine has run, fire up your browser and go to `http://localhost:8080/Navigator`, or if you want to connect from a remote machine on your network go to `http://ip_address_of_seewhy_server:8080/Navigator`. Either way, you should be asked to log in, to which you can use **seewhy** as both the username and password and you will then be presented with a screen like this:

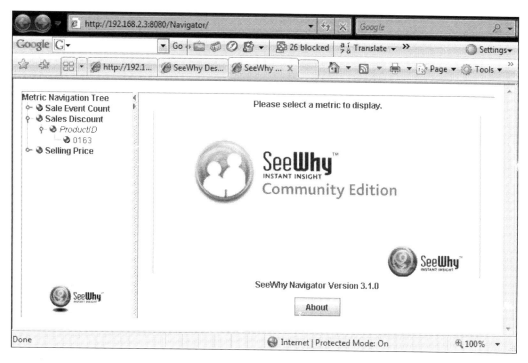

Set up the BAM points on the graph

With SeeWhy successfully installed, we now need to get jBPM talking to it. For the purposes of getting this up and running, we are going to keep this very simple, merely counting the number of times a particular task node is hit. We will experiment with SeeWhy later in this chapter to track metrics that are more meaningful in our process environment.

We will track the number of times the `Select band members` task node in our process definition is hit by an instance of the process. To do this, we need to modify our process definition, so start up the Designer. We will change our process definition to include a new node that will notify the SeeWhy software to increase its count of `Select band members` tasks by one each time the process comes through. To do this, we add a new node called `Call SeeWhy`, immediately after the `Select band members` node and join the process definition back up:

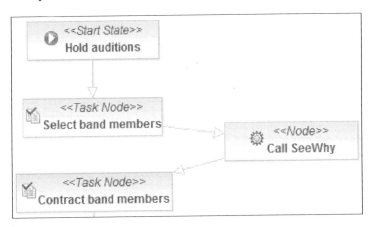

Note that we have just used a plain old node of type "node", not a task node, as we are simply using it as a container for an action rather than asking someone to do some work here. This call to SeeWhy will use a custom action handler, in a similar fashion to what we did previously for our integration with the Royalties database. This action handler will get the information from the `Select band members` node and pass it on through to SeeWhy in the form of a JMS message.

 JMS, or the "Java Messaging Service", is the standard method for sending and receiving interface messages between applications in a Java environment. In other words, it is a technology Java applications use to talk to each other.

In the Package Explorer, navigate to the `src/main/java` folder, right-click and select **New | Package**. Give the new package a name of `com.seewhy.jbpm`. Right-click your new package and select **Import**. Select to import from **File System**, then browse to the location on your hard drive where you have unzipped the code download for this chapter. Locate the two files in the download called `MessageSender.java` and `SeeWhyExternalMessageSender.java`: check the boxes next to these two files and click **Finish**.

When you do this the `SeeWhyExternalMessageSender.java` file may well show a little red cross next to it in the Package Explorer indicating that there is a problem with it. Not to worry, this is easily solved: the Java class has been written to comply with the 1.5 version of the Java development kit and Eclipse may be configured to work with 1.4. To fix the problem, in Eclipse, go into the **Window** menu, then to **Preferences**. Navigate the preferences tree to the **Java/Compiler** node. In the **Compiler compliance level** field, select "1.5". The project should rebuild itself and we should lose our error message. You may be left with some warning notifications but don't worry about these.

Now go into the Outline view, find the new `Call SeeWhy` node, right-click and select **Add Actions | Node Enter**. Double-click the `action1` action that is added to the node and switch to the **Handler** dialog. In the **Class** field, enter the path to our new action handler: `com.seewhy.jbpm.MessageSender`, then in the field configuration dialog check the `myEventName` **Field Name** and specify `SelectBandMember` for its **Field Value** (notice that we've run the words together). Secondly, specify `bm1`,`bm2`,`bm3`,`bm4`,`bm5`,`bm6` for the `myVariablesToUse` field: leave the `myDisableSend` unchecked, it's there for debugging purposes:

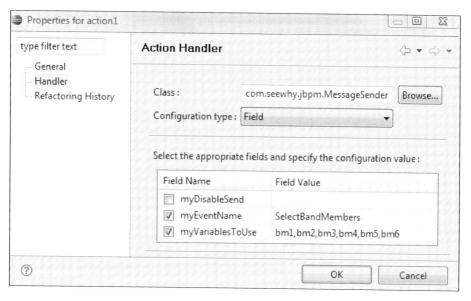

With our process definition amended, we just need to deploy it to the server. Start up the database and then JBoss, then deploy the process definition and the action handler code to the server: we've done this enough times by now, I'm sure you know how to do it!

Make the action handler code available to jBPM

It is a slight quirk of jBPM that in order to make our SeeWhy action handler code available to our process definition, we need to actually deploy it within the web console package itself. The first step in doing this is to export the action handler code from Eclipse as a `.jar` file. In the Package Explorer, navigate to the `com.seewhy.jbpm` node of the `src/main/java` tree. Right-click on this node and select **Export**. In the **Export** dialog, expand the **Java** node and choose **JAR file**, then click **Next**. In the next screen, make sure the `com.seewhy.jbpm` package is checked for export and export the file to your desktop with a name of **com-seewhy-jbpm.jar**:

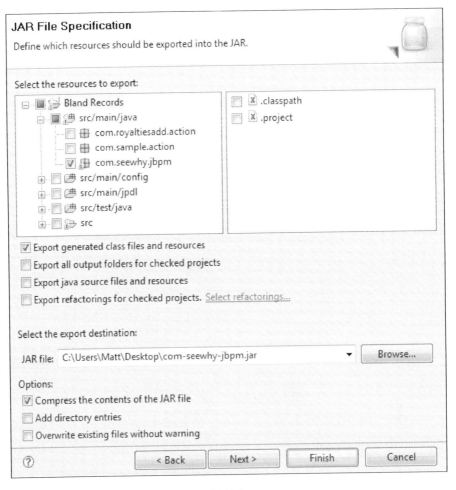

Click **Finish** to complete the export. You may get some warning messages but these can be safely ignored. If you now look at your desktop, you should find the new `com-seewhy-jbpm.jar` file; now we need to add this to our web console package. As we did earlier in this chapter when we swapped out the web console logo, we need to extract the `jbpm-console.war` file to a temporary location with a handy ZIP utility. When this is done, navigate to the `WEB-INF\lib` folder and copy in our `com-seewhy-jbpm.jar` file:

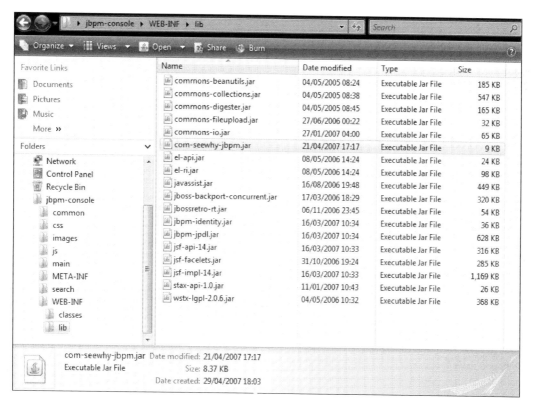

With our code safely accessible to the web console, all we need to do now is re-war the package and deploy it to the server. Open up the command line, use the `CD` command to navigate to the top level of your temporary `jbpm-console` directory, and then use the following command to create a new `.war` file:

```
jar cMf jbpm-console.war *
```

Copy the resulting `jbpm-console.war` file into the `deploy` directory of your jBPM JBoss installation to complete the process.

Configure the jBPM JBoss server

Now, we need to configure a JMS queue so that the server knows where to send the messages that will be output as a result of hitting the `Call SeeWhy` node. We are going to put our event message on an outbound message queue, where it will be picked up by the SeeWhy JBoss server.

To set up the jBPM JMS queue, find the `jbpm-seewhy-jms-service.xml` file in the code download for this chapter and put it into the `deploy\jms` folder of your jBPM Boss server installation: for me this is at `C:\Users\Matt\jBPM\jbpm-jpdl-3.2.GA\ server\server\jbpm\deploy\jms`. If you open up this file in Notepad, you can see that is quite simple and just tells the server about the queue that we are going to use called `"jBPMSourceQueue"`.

```xml
<?xml version="1.0" encoding="UTF-8"?>

<server>
 <mbean code="org.jboss.mq.server.jmx.Queue" name="jboss.
mq.destination:service=Queue,name=jBPMSourceQueue">
     <depends optional-attribute-name="DestinationManager">jboss.mq:
service=DestinationManager</depends>
     <depends optional-attribute-name="SecurityManager">jboss.mq:
service=SecurityManager</depends>
   </mbean>
</server>
```

That's it, the jBPM side of the equation is set up and ready to go. Note that we have configured our setup in such a way as to have jBPM post its messages locally for the remote SeeWhy machine to pick up. We could easily have set this up the other way round if we preferred, with jBPM putting its messages on the SeeWhy machine. To do this, we'd need to create a `jndi.properties` file describing the name and location of the remote JMS queue and alter the jBPM JBoss start server command to include a reference to this file (with something like `-DSeeWhyJNDIProperties="C:/ jndi.properties"`). Of course, the two components could also be co-located in the same JBoss instance, if that made sense in your environment. We won't linger over the details of this as the setup we are going for is perfectly fine.

Telling SeeWhy about our process event

With the jBPM side set up, now we need to get the SeeWhy installation looking in the right place and ready to receive data when we execute the process. The first step is to build an event schema file that defines the structure of the business events that SeeWhy will receive. We need to specify the name that we are using for our business event, as well as picking out any variables we might be interested in and that are available through the process context. If you remember we configured our action handler to pick up the `bmx` variables and put them into the event message for us.

In our schema file, we need to specify what kind of variables we are expecting: basically, we use `CodeType` if we're expecting text and `MeasureType` if we are expecting numbers. In the code download for this chapter, you will find a file called `SelectBandMembers.xsd`. Copy this file to the `projectschemas.war` folder under your `deploy` directory in the SeeWhy JBoss installation. If you open up the file in a text editor you can see what it contains:

```
<?xml version="1.0" encoding="UTF-8"?>
<!-- Written by: SeeWhy Software -->

<xs:schema xmlns:xs="http://www.w3.org/2001/XMLSchema" xmlns:
cct="http://www.seewhy.com/2003/1/cct" xmlns:cyt="http://www.seewhy.
com/2003/1/systemtypes" elementFormDefault="qualified" attributeFormDe
fault="unqualified">
    <xs:import namespace="http://www.seewhy.com/2003/1/systemtypes"
schemaLocation="http://localhost:8080/coreschemas/SeeWhySystemTypes.
xsd"/>
    <xs:element name="SelectBandMembers">
       <xs:annotation>

<xs:documentation>SelectBandMembers</xs:documentation>
       </xs:annotation>
       <xs:complexType>
          <xs:complexContent>
             <xs:extension base="cyt:BusinessEventType">
                <xs:sequence>
                   <xs:element name="bm1" type="cct:CodeType"/>
                   <xs:element name="bm2" type="cct:CodeType"/>
                   <xs:element name="bm3" type="cct:CodeType"/>
                   <xs:element name="bm4" type="cct:CodeType"/>
                   <xs:element name="bm5" type="cct:CodeType"/>
                   <xs:element name="bm6" type="cct:CodeType"/>
                </xs:sequence>
             </xs:extension>
          </xs:complexContent>
       </xs:complexType>
    </xs:element>
</xs:schema>
```

One further amendment that we need to make in this folder is to open up the `eventList.txt` file and add in an entry of `SelectBandMembers` to the end, like this:

```
Sale
SelectBandMembers
```

Now SeeWhy knows about the type of event that we are going to send it from jBPM.

Configuring SeeWhy's incoming event interface

Next, we need to set up a SeeWhy event interface and assimilator. These elements are the technical configuration of the SeeWhy components that actually receive the events and pass them to SeeWhy's Interpretation engine.

Setting up SeeWhy to receive the jBPM message queue is a relatively simple matter. In your SeeWhy installation, find the `SeeWhy_Scripts` folder in the `SeeWhy_Tutorial` directory. In here, you will see a file called `createEventScripts.bat`: double-click it. This handy little utility will create the basics of the configuration files we need to get SeeWhy looking in the right place. You will be prompted to enter a name for the event: enter `SelectBandMembers` as we used in our action handler. You will also be prompted for the name of the event schema file; just hit **Enter** again to use the default. The utility program will then create the files that we need in a new `event_SelectBandMembers` folder. There is a bit of tweaking we need to do before this will work, however.

The first thing we have to do is change the `SelectBandMembers_EventDataFeed.properties` file, as it is set up to read from a local message queue and we want to get our events from the remote jBPM queue. In the default version of the `SelectBandMembers_EventDataFeed.properties`, you will see three properties that point straight back to this file: `HandShakeConstructorProperties`, `PayloadTransformerProperties`, and `PluggableEventFeedProperties`. It is the last of these we are interested in as it defines the queue from which we are expecting to get our event details. Change the line:

```
PluggableEventFeedProperties=./event_SelectBandMembers/
SelectBandMembers_EventDataFeed.properties
```

to:

```
PluggableEventFeedProperties=./event_SelectBandMembers/InboundJMS.
properties
```

You will also see some lines a bit further down that look like this:

```
#JMSEventSystem.properties
#
EventQueueJNDI=queue/eventjBPMSeeWhyQueue
```

Remove this bit of code: we are going to specify our own JMS event system properties in a separate file. Speaking of which, find the `InboundJMS.properties` file in the chapter's download. This file defines the JMS queue that the SeeWhy JBoss server is going to connect to:

```
#JMSEventSystem.properties
#
EventQueueJNDI=queue/jBPMSourceQueue
HandShakeConstructorProperties=SelectBandMembers_JMSEventDataFeed.
properties

#EventDataFeed.properties
#JMSEventSystem.properties
#
ConnectionFactoryJNDI=ConnectionFactory
JNDIProperties=jms-jndi.properties
```

Put the `InboundJMS.properties` file in the same folder as our `SelectBandMembers_EventDataFeed.properties` file: for me, this is at `C:\SeeWhy Community Edition V3.2\SeeWhy_Tutorial\SeeWhy_Scripts\event_SelectBandMembers`.

To complete our connection between the two servers, we need to make sure that the SeeWhy JBoss server recognizes the location of the remote jBPM JBoss server. To do this, we need to put a `.properties` file in the `SeeWhy_Scripts` folder of our SeeWhy installation. In the download for the chapter, you'll find a file called `jms-jndi.properties`. Open this up in Notepad, and edit the line that specifies the location of the jBPM server: note that this must end in "`:1099`" as that is the server port that we need to connect to with JMS. For me, this file looks like this:

```
java.naming.factory.initial=org.jnp.interfaces.NamingContextFactory
java.naming.factory.url.pkgs=org.jboss.naming:org.jnp.interfaces
java.naming.provider.url=jnp://192.168.2.4:1099
```

Save this file into the `SeeWhy_Scripts` folder: for me, this is at `C:\SeeWhy Community Edition V3.2\SeeWhy_Tutorial\SeeWhy_Scripts\`.

Now let's see if all our configuration work has paid off. Start the database servers on both machines, then start both JBoss servers. If you have no errors reported by the startup routines, double-click the `SelectBandMembers_run_EIandAssim.bat` file to start the event interface and the assimilator. All being well, the command-line console should show something like the following:

```
PayloadTransformerInterface implementation.
EventInterface 20:42:17,598 INFO  [SAXXMLPayloadTransformer] Parser class is: co
m.bluecast.xml.JAXPSAXParserFactory$JAXPSAXParser
EventInterface 20:42:17,598 INFO  [SAXXMLPayloadTransformer] Initialized Payload
TransformerInterface implementation.
EventInterface 20:42:17,598 INFO  [EventDataFeed] Initialized the PayloadTransfo
rmer.
EventInterface 20:42:17,598 INFO  [EventDataFeed] About to initialize and start
the PluggableEventFeed.
EventInterface 20:42:17,608 INFO  [JMSEventSystem] About to initialize DataFeedE
ventInterface implementation.
EventInterface 20:42:17,608 WARN  [a] DataFailureLoggingLocation is not defined
- so will write where ever we're running from
EventInterface 20:42:17,608 WARN  [a] DataFailureFilePrefix is not defined - so
output name will not be meaningful
EventInterface 20:42:17,608 INFO  [JMSEventSystem] About to connect to Event Que
ue.
EventInterface 20:42:17,608 INFO  [b] Got InitialContext.
EventInterface 20:42:17,608 INFO  [b] About to get QueueConnectionFactory.
EventInterface 20:42:17,608 INFO  [b] JNDI Factory name - ConnectionFactory
EventInterface 20:42:17,679 INFO  [b] Got QueueConnectionFactory.
EventInterface 20:42:17,679 INFO  [JMSEventSystem] About to get QueueConnection.

EventInterface 20:42:17,709 INFO  [JMSEventSystem] Got QueueConnection.
EventInterface 20:42:17,709 INFO  [JMSEventSystem] About to create QueueSession.

EventInterface 20:42:17,709 INFO  [JMSEventSystem] Created QueueSession.
EventInterface 20:42:17,709 INFO  [b] About to look up queue, property name: Eve
ntQueueJNDI
EventInterface 20:42:17,719 INFO  [b] Looked up queue, property name: EventQueue
JNDI
EventInterface 20:42:17,719 INFO  [JMSEventSystem] About to create QueueReceiver
.
EventInterface 20:42:17,729 INFO  [JMSEventSystem] Created QueueReceiver.
EventInterface 20:42:17,729 INFO  [b] About to close InitialContext.
EventInterface 20:42:17,729 INFO  [b] Closed InitialContext.
EventInterface 20:42:17,729 INFO  [JMSEventSystem] Connected to Event Queue.
EventInterface 20:42:17,729 INFO  [JMSEventSystem] Initialized DataFeedEventInte
rface implementation.
EventInterface 20:42:17,729 INFO  [JMSEventSystem] About to accept subscriber.
EventInterface 20:42:17,729 INFO  [JMSEventSystem] Subscriber accepted.
EventInterface 20:42:17,729 INFO  [JMSEventSystem] About to begin handling event
s.
EventInterface 20:42:17,729 INFO  [JMSEventSystem] About to set MessageListener.

EventInterface 20:42:17,729 INFO  [JMSEventSystem] Set MessageListener.
EventInterface 20:42:17,729 INFO  [JMSEventSystem] About to start Connection.
EventInterface 20:42:17,729 INFO  [JMSEventSystem] Started Connection.
EventInterface 20:42:17,729 INFO  [JMSEventSystem] Begun handling events.
EventInterface 20:42:17,729 INFO  [EventDataFeed] Initialized and started the Pl
uggableEventFeed. Class identified by config is com.seewhy.eventinterface.EventC
hannels.JMSTransport.JMSEventSystem
EventInterface 20:42:17,729 INFO  [EventDataFeed] About to initialize the PostPa
rsedDataTransformers.
EventInterface 20:42:17,729 INFO  [EventDataFeed] Initalized 0 PostParsedDataTra
nsformers.
EventInterface 20:42:17,729 INFO  [EventDataFeed] Started the EventDataFeed.
```

That should be it, but let's just check that it is working. Fire up the jBPM web console and go through the process up to and beyond the `Select Band Members` node. You shouldn't have any problems getting past the node. Now go to **Start | All Programs | MySQL | MySQL Server 5.0 | MySQL Command Line Client**. Enter the password for your MySQL server. At the `mysql>` prompt, type `use seewhy`. With the database selected, type the following SQL to see if our event has come across:

```
SELECT * FROM cyeSelectBandMembers;
```

You should get an output that shows the table does have an event in there (I have two in mine):

```
MySQL Command Line Client                                        _ □ ×
Enter password: *******
Welcome to the MySQL monitor.  Commands end with ; or \g.
Your MySQL connection id is 13 to server version: 5.0.15-nt

Type 'help;' or '\h' for help. Type '\c' to clear the buffer.

mysql> use seewhy
Database changed
mysql> SELECT * FROM cyeSelectBandMembers;
+-----------------+--------+--------+--------+--------+--------+--------+--------+--------+--------+
| EventGUID                              | bm5   | EventName         | EventDateT
ime | bm2   | bm1   | bm3    | EventReceivedDateTime | bm4 | bm6   | Even
tSource                        | Id |
+-----------------+--------+--------+--------+--------+--------+--------+--------+--------+--------+
| 393cd0c3-c0a8-0203-00d9-0453722204d9 | asdfsf | SelectBandMembers | 1177780277
173 | asdfs | bmnbm | asfdd  |          1177781325989 | asdf | asfdsafd | 192.
168.2.3:JMS_SelectBandMembers |  1 |
| 393e4e8f-c0a8-0203-0073-8d088d6ef5d8 | bmnbmn | SelectBandMembers | 1177781421
759 | bmb   | bma   | bob colin |       1177781423749 | bmx | bmnbnb   | 192.
168.2.3:JMS_SelectBandMembers |  2 |
+-----------------+--------+--------+--------+--------+--------+--------+--------+--------+--------+

2 rows in set (0.00 sec)

mysql>
```

Congratulations, our two JBoss servers are now talking to each other!

If the database isn't populated, you need to look around to see what's gone wrong. A couple of things to check straight off are:

Is everything named correctly? If you make a spelling mistake in the queue names, event schema name, and so on, it won't work.

Check the CY-EventStreamLog.log log file in the SeeWhy installation folders. This contains a log of activity from the Event Interface and Assimilator: you should see some indicators of activity there. If not, your Event Interface and Assimilator setup isn't working at all.

Tell SeeWhy how to interpret the data

With our interface between SeeWhy and jBPM up and running, we must now tell SeeWhy how we want it to interpret the data that comes through. To do this, we need to define metric calculations and rules using the SeeWhy Desktop. This will determine what happens to the content of the events that we will capture in the Interpretation engine.

Go to `http://your-server-ip:8080/Desktop` and click **Metric Configuration** at the top of the Desktop. Put in an ID of "**SelectBandMemberCount**", a name of "**SelectBandMember Count**", and a description of, yes, you guessed it, "**Count of SelectBandMember**":

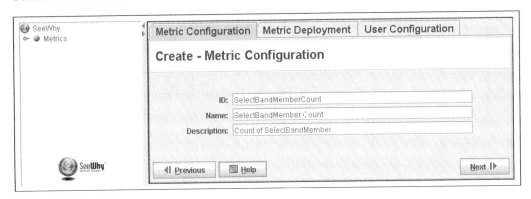

Click **Next**. In the next screen, click **Configure** in the **Value** field. In the **Functions** dialog, browse down to **COUNT()** and double-click it. Then in the **Events** dialog, browse down to our **SelectBandMembers** event and double-click that. You'll notice how the metric expression builds up at the top of the screen and that the validity of this expression is evaluated at the bottom. In the **Parameters** dialog, highlight **SelectBandMembers** and click **Configure**. In the resulting window, for the **Parameter Types** field choose **Aggregation**:

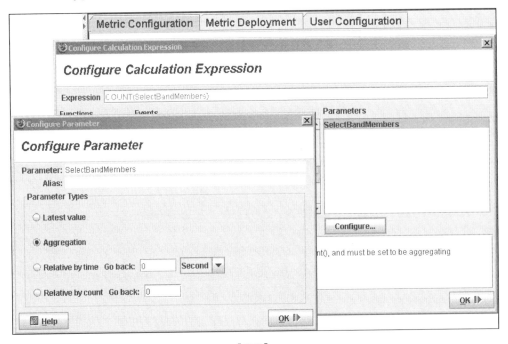

Click **OK**. In the **Aggregation Period** field, choose **1 Minute**: although this is a very short time period, it will at least allow us to see the data going through the system fairly easily (our resulting graph will make some sense when we put some test data through: the aggregation means that the count won't endlessly increase as you might assume). Make sure the **Record** box is flagged. In the **Triggers** field, click **Configure**. Check the box next to **SelectBandMembers** and click **OK**:

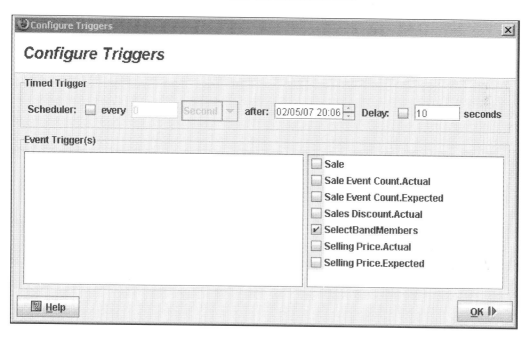

The trigger simply tells SeeWhy which incoming event to look out for with this particular metric. Click **Next** then **Next** again. SeeWhy should confirm that our metric has been created; now we must deploy it. Click the **Metric Deployment** tab and choose the "**Deploy metrics from work area to live**" option. Click **Next**. SeeWhy should confirm that our metric has been deployed. To see the metric, we need to go to the SeeWhy Navigator. Go to `http://your-server-ip:8080/Navigator/` in your browser. You will notice that our metric doesn't appear in the list of metrics on the left of the screen yet: we need to run some new data through first, as only those metrics for which SeeWhy has calculated data will appear in the Navigator.

Go back into the jBPM console on the other machine and start a new instance of the process. Go through the process until and beyond the `Select Band Members` node. Do this a few times so that there is some data running through. Now go back to the Navigator: our metric should now show up, and we should just about be able to see some data in the far right of the graph:

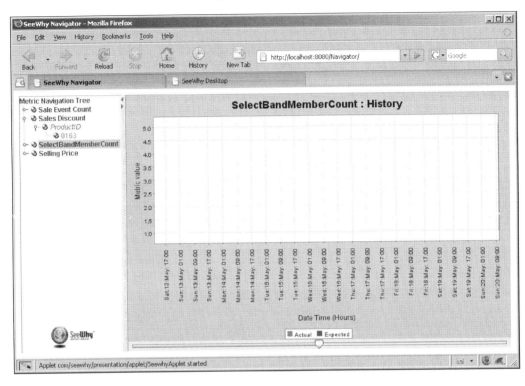

Position your cursor over the slash of red that indicates your metric data on the graph, right-click, and choose **Zoom In | Horizontal Axis**. Do this a few times until the data becomes clearly visible:

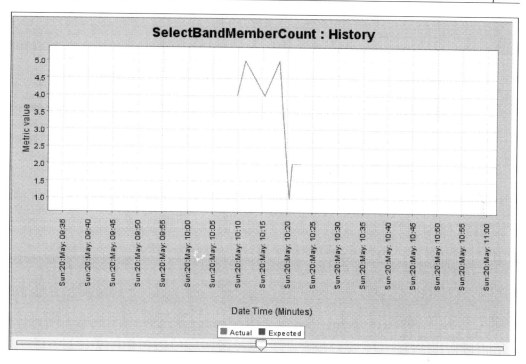

Congratulations, you now have data flowing through your BAM solution!

Taking it further

There are many options for configuring SeeWhy to meet our specific needs. As this book isn't a SeeWhy tutorial, we won't go into a great deal of detail, although let's point out a few key features that we'll probably want to take advantage of:

- Functions: SeeWhy has a whole host of inbuilt functions that we can use to transform the incoming data. We have seen the COUNT() function in our example above, but there are many others for us to play around with. AVERAGE(), MAX(), MIN(), and SUM() are some of the more obvious ones.

- Dimensions: Our action handler that we have implemented in jBPM will pass over all the process variables that we specify in our event schema. This allows us to dimension our process metric according to each of those process variables. It doesn't make much sense in the example we did above (who would be interested in seeing the count of the number of times we've hit Select Band Members per bmx process variable?), but clearly this would be valuable in other situations. For instance, we might well be interested in tracking the positive response rate on contract negotiations and this could be done by using the ContractAgreed process variables as dimensions.

- Users: we'll need to set up our managers or team leaders as users so they can access SeeWhy and start acting on the information it is providing them. This is easily done in the User Configuration aspect of the Desktop.

There are many more options open to us: please review the tutorial, reference, and guide documents in your SeeWhy installation folder for more details, as well as the ever-growing amount of support material on the SeeWhy website at `http://www.seewhy.com`.

Set up email notifications

Not only can SeeWhy report on data, it can also send out notifications via email to our users to let them know about things going on during process execution. These email notifications are triggered by process metrics moving beyond a pre-defined range of "normal" data.

Tell SeeWhy when to alert

Currently, our metrics are calculating values but don't have any rules behind them to tell SeeWhy when to send an alert to the user: this is the first thing we need to add. Let's edit the configuration of the `SelectBandMemberCount` metric to set up a rule. In the Desktop, open up the **Metric Configuration** aspect. Select the **Modify existing metric** option then click **Next**. The next panel will show a field with the metric name greyed out. Select **Metrics** in the left-hand tree so it is expanded, you can then see the available metrics including our `SelectBandMemberCount` metric. Click the `SelectBandMemberCount` metric in the tree and that metric name will appear in the grey field in the centre of the display and will be checked in the tree. Click **Edit** then **Next**.

In the **Modify – Configure Actual Calculation: SelectBandMemberCount** panel we want to set a simple threshold at which point an alert will be generated. To do this, check the box next to the **Thresholds** field and then click the **Configure...** button. This will open a new dialog called **Configure Thresholds**.

To illustrate the basic principles, we'll set the **Lower Threshold** to "-1" and the **Upper Threshold** to "1" and check the **Always Trigger** checkbox. This means that every time our count exceeds 1 within our aggregate time, (which if you remember was set to one minute) we will get an alert for each calculation performed with a result above 1. If the calculation was able to drop below -1 then we'd also see an alert when the lower threshold was passed: although obviously this would not be possible in our scenario. To get this into effect, we need to OK the dialog (the **Thresholds** field will now contain a textual description of the limits we've just defined). Then press the **Save** button.

Thresholds:	☑	Alert state 1 when above 1.0
		Alert state 0 when between 1.0 and -1.0
		Alert state 1 when below -1.0

Once saved, in the same way as when we first created the metric, it needs to be deployed to the server.

Configure a notification

The first thing we have to do is to create or obtain a template that can be used to create the notification. Fortunately, an example template has been already created and is included in the SeeWhy installation. We can use the `aggalertmail.html` and `aggalertmailsubject.txt` files that can be found at `C:\SeeWhy Community Edition V3.2\SeeWhy_Tutorial\SeeWhy_Mail\Mail_Templates`. You will see a couple of other example templates in there as well.

Now select the **User Configuration** aspect. The left-hand tree will show the known users and notifications that are available. We have to connect our metric up to the notification template that is to be used and then to then the channel through which the notification should be sent. On the tree, right-click on **Notifications** and choose **New**. This will give us a panel for defining the notification. We need to start by defining the **Alert Reference**: this links us to the metric. So select the **Configure...** button, which will pop up a new dialog. Select the **SelectBandMemberCount** metric from the drop-down box. The remaining settings don't need to be changed for this basic example, so the dialog can be closed with the **OK** button. The **Alert Reference** field will now show **SelectBandMemberCount.Rule.Actual**, which means SeeWhy will send out a notification every time the threshold we set previously is broken by the "actual" calculated value of the incoming data.

We can leave the **Alert State** and **Media** fields to their defaults. Finally, we need to select our notification templates: `aggalertmailsubject.txt` for the header and `aggalertmail.html` for the body. Complete the process by clicking the **Save** button.

Before anyone can receive a notification, they need a suitable address, for us just an email address. As we're going to use the JAMES email server that SeeWhy has installed for us, and we're the default `seewhy` user, we need to make sure that the `seewhy` user has a suitable email address. To do this, we need to open up the **Users** part of the tree and select **seewhy | User Contacts**. Click **Add** in the bottom right-hand corner and add in an email address of **seewhy@localhost.localdomain**, then **OK** the dialog. The email address will appear in the list and we can save that change.

The last step is to tell SeeWhy which notifications we're interested in. Select the **User Subscriptions** element for the `seewhy` user. We need to **Add** a new subscription (each subscription we have appears in the list). The **Add** button opens a new dialog where we choose the **Alert Reference** again using the **Configure…** button. This provides us with a dialog just like the **Notification Definition** one, so we need to enter the same values: choose **SelectBandMemberCount** from the dropdown and close with the **OK** button. In our scenario, it is only really meaningful when the alert starts (or continues to be on) so we can select **On** for the **Alert State** and close the dialog with the **OK** button. The list will now contain a description of our new subscription that we just need to save using the **Save** button.

Setting up your email client

To be able to receive the notification emails, an email client will need to be able to receive email from the local mail server JAMES (note that you could also configure SeeWhy to talk to your own mail server). Open Outlook and click **Tools**. Select **Account Settings** then click **New** in **Email Accounts**. Select **POP3** then **Next**. Set the **Your Name** field to **seewhy** with an email address of **seewhy@localhost.localdomain**, a user name of **seewhy**, and a password of **seewhy**. Incoming and outgoing mail server should both be **localhost**. If you have the mail server running, you can click on **Test Account Settings** to make sure you're set up correctly. To start the server, double-click the `Start E-mail Server.bat` file in the `SeeWhy_Tutorial` folder. OK the dialogs in Outlook to complete the setup.

Testing the notifications

With all the changes made, we need to go back to the jBPM web console and work through more than one process instance per minute to trigger the alert. The alert may take a little while to appear in your email client, depending upon timing settings on your email client, but it will eventually get there:

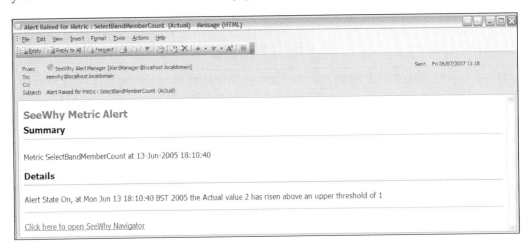

As you can see, this is fairly straightforward, but does at least show the concept in action. The SeeWhy notification template syntax gives us lots of opportunities to improve on this basic format though, and with a bit of work we can end up with something as good-looking and complex as this example:

From: SeeWhy Alert Manager [eng_test1@seewhy.com]
Sent: 25 April 2007 11:18
To: alert_manager@seewhy.com
Subject: Store: 3120, Alert for Cashier : 12894240, Metric: NoSale Alert

Transaction No Sale Alert for Cashier 12894240

An alert has been raised at 25 April 2007 11:18:11 because Cashier (12894240) has changed their No Sale behaviour in the last 24 hours, and No Sales are now significantly higher than in the past.

Cashier Statistics for 12894240 in the last 24 hours:

Total Transactions	172	No Of Voided Transactions	3
No of Line Voids	2	No of Voided Transactions over £200	1
No of Sales Overrings	0	No of Refund Overrings	0
No of NoSales	12	No of Refunds	12
No of Transactions under 30p	0	No of Tills Used	3

Cashier Statistics for 12894240 the last 30 days:

Average Transactions	947.55	Average No Of Voided Transactions	9.34
Average No of NoSales	1.39		

Average Cashier Statistics for this Store the last 30 days:

Average Transactions	1,125	Average No Of Voided Transactions	8.91
Average No of NoSales	0.8		

Store Statistics for the last 30 days:

Total Transactions	374,281	No Of Voided Transactions	3,960
No of Line Voids	18,309	No of Voided Transactions over £200	13
No of Sales Overrings	86	No of Refund Overrings	11
No of NoSales	548	No of Refunds	21,594
No of Transactions under 30p	564	No of Cashier Used	395

Last 20 NoSales for this cashier

Date & Time	Store	Cashier	Till	Type ID	NoSale	Fill Form ID	Till Type	No. Sales	Total Value £	Total After Checking £	Total Amount Tendered	Cash Back Value
Tue 23rd Apr 18:56:31	3120	12894240	343	32703214	Y	#336	9	0	£.0.00	£0.00	£0.00	£0.00
Tue 23rd Apr 18:43:50	3120	12894240	343	32703214	Y	#336	9	0	£.0.00	£0.00	£0.00	£0.00
Tue 23rd Apr 18:26:50	3120	12894240	343	32703214	Y	#336	9	0	£.0.00	£0.00	£0.00	£0.00

Using SeeWhy for BAM

Now that we've seen the basics of SeeWhy, how are we going to apply it to our Business Activity Monitoring requirement? The following paragraphs set out some ideas:

- Process management: we've already seen how SeeWhy is great for alerting our users to abnormal events that happen during process execution. Clearly, we are going to be able to configure metrics that allow us to track time overruns, delays, and bottlenecks based on comparisons with average, minimum or maximum process data. More often than not, this is going to involve tracking two events: we'll need to be calculating the time elapsed from when a process instance enters a node to when it leaves it. From this, we will be able to derive extremely accurate activity and process cycle time.

- Process metrics analysis: having identified the primary process metrics that we're going to track early on in our project, it is simply a matter of configuring them in SeeWhy and then using the default Navigator screens. For instance, one of the most expensive activities we identified during our analysis phase was that of "Write songs". If we configure a process metric to track the cycle time of this activity, we will be able to see the long term trend using averages over an aggregated period and we can focus on driving it down.

- Process forecasting: using process metrics trend analysis techniques SeeWhy can identify "expected" values given past process metrics calculations. For instance, we would be able to calculate the average time it will take to finish the activity from the current point in the process. SeeWhy can calculate expected values for any process metric it tracks, so the possibilities are endless.

There is a great deal to discover and put to use in the SeeWhy business intelligence platform, and we have merely scratched the surface of what's possible: we could write a whole book about it. Nevertheless, hopefully this part of the book has given you some ideas and pointers for how it can become a vital part of your end-to-end BPM suite.

Go-live

Our BPM system is now officially a BPM "suite" and is in a state of readiness for go-live. All that remains is for us to obtain final sign-off from our stakeholders and our sponsors. Then it is simply a matter of following our detailed implementation plan. When we do put the new system live, it is important that we don't get sidetracked by the million and one "good ideas" that are bound to arise as a result of us letting loose a bunch of new users on the system. The Business Analyst's favorite weapon has always been "prioritization" and this will be an excellent time to put it into practice.

After all, with the system now live we are no longer in the development phase: anything that comes up now is a change request for a live system. Change requests should be prioritized according to the business case for the change and a decision on their validity taken by some kind of review board.

Now that our system is live, we are ready for the final stage of our BPM project: ongoing process improvement. Our project sponsor is likely to be pleased, because this is the part of the project that is likely to deliver the biggest return on our investment. We'll tackle this in the next and final chapter.

Summary

This has been one of our more technical chapters, although hopefully we haven't lost you along the way! Even if we have, this chapter will still have showed you what it is possible to accomplish with jBPM and other related toolsets. We have taken our system from a bare-bones business process management proof-of-concept system to a mature and robust BPM suite. Now, it is time to capitalize on all our hard work and start getting a return from our investment. Our work force will now be better organized and more productive, and we as Business Analysts can start analyzing the data coming out of our BPM system to see where we can make further process improvements.

In this chapter, we have:

- Considered what should go into a detailed implementation plan
- Changed the database back end of jBPM for something more robust
- Developed a process monitoring solution for our BPM suite

7
Ongoing process improvement

As the sun sets on our glorious BPM project, it is time to look back in wonder at the highs and lows that got us this far. Is our sponsor happy? Have our users adopted the system? How much has the application saved our business? The answers to these questions may not always be positive, but they must be posed if we are to learn for next time. And just as we reach what we believe to be the summit of this particular project mountain, we find that this is in fact, only the first in a series of peaks, leading to a much higher pinnacle. In fact, the work has only just begun. The real improvements are still to come from ongoing process improvement efforts based on the high quality process metrics data we are now collecting. JBoss jBPM is such a rich product that it would be churlish to stop at what we have got now: there are many opportunities for further development that remain to be explored.

In this final chapter we will:

- Assess our project
- Perform process analysis and ongoing improvement
- Put together business process documentation
- Present ideas for further development of our BPM system

Project assessment

No project runs smoothly from start to finish: if it did, there would be no need for talented people like us to fix the problems. Along the way, we have probably pulled some clever stunts to make sure we got the right result. Now that the project is over, the really clever thing to do is look back and make sure we don't find ourselves facing the same issues next time.

We shouldn't concentrate on the mistakes and ignore our successes, however. With our business process management system in place, our sponsor happy, and our users over the moon with their shiny new tool, it's time to back up this feel-good moment with some hard numbers: how much money has our system saved the company?

Having completed our project review, it is time to retire the project team and move into business as usual mode.

Project post mortem

The atmosphere in a project post mortem often lives up to its name. It can be a painful exercise in blame and counter-blame. Sometimes, this is unavoidable: if a member of the team really hasn't performed then they must be held accountable. However, a strong project manager would ensure a non-performing team member was removed from the project before the project was over. It is a defining characteristic of the project post mortem that responsibility for both the successes and failures of the project are apportioned among the team. This is a valuable exercise, as it allows those team members to recognize those areas where they are strong versus those areas where they are weaker and could improve.

Aside from producing learning points for individuals, it is important that the organization as a whole learns from the experience. After all, it may be a completely different set of people who take on the next BPM implementation project. The first and probably most important action that the team can take is to make sure the project's documentation is fully squared away and properly archived. When that new team of BPM implementers come to start their project in a year's time, they should be able to look back at our documentation and see the full story of how the project unfolded. We must make sure our code is well documented and the system architecture is properly modeled. The new team should also be able to read a document that sets out the specific "learning points for next time" that we have identified.

This part of the project lifecycle is so often overlooked that it is practically unheard of for it to happen properly. Nevertheless, it cannot be stressed enough how valuable it can be. Project managers should get ready for a fight with management who will almost certainly want to roll the team onto a new project as soon as the system has gone live. Good luck!

Evaluate project versus success criteria

With the project over and the system in use, at a certain point it pays to perform some retrospective analysis about how successful our project has been. Have we done what we said we were going to do? If we have, then great, let's see what else we can achieve. If we haven't, let's see what we can do to turn the situation around and get back on track. Of course, we can't do this kind of assessment immediately after going live: any new system and process takes a certain amount of time to bed in. Sometimes, it can take many months for a user community to get over its initial inertia and get used to a new way of working.

Way back in Chapter 2 we defined what our success criteria for this project would be and when they should be assessed. To save you looking back through the book, let's repeat them here:

- The process time from first audition to album release is reduced from six months to four.

- Pipeline can be forecasted and controlled, so that competing products from Bland Records are not released on the market at exactly the same time.

- The above success criteria will be assessed six months after implementation of the project in order to allow the changes to take effect.

Let's look at each of these in turn.

Firstly, have we reduced the process time from first audition to album release? Well obviously, this is a simulated example, so without setting up a new company called Bland Records there is no way we can assess this criterion. Nevertheless, in a real-life scenario this would probably be a very crucial measure of our project's success, and should be relatively easy to gauge. Reducing the turnaround time of an end-to-end process is one of the key promises of a BPM implementation and if we haven't made any progress on this, then we should be pretty worried that something has gone wrong somewhere. Obviously, make sure you have left enough time between implementing the system and conducting the assessment for the process to have taken a "clean" turn through its cycle; otherwise you will get a result that is skewed because of a hangover from the old way of working.

Our second success criterion can be judged for our example scenario. We have indeed made it possible to predict Bland's pipeline and for management to adjust the process output so that releases do not clash in the same month. The reports we put together with our SeeWhy implementation in the last chapter, are a great way for Mr Gali to maintain visibility over his pipeline. From these reports, it is a simple matter to delay or bring forward a particular instance of the process by the managers prioritizing or de-prioritizing it in the web console. They could even simply tell a user not to process a particular instance until a certain date. Either way, control over the pipeline is achieved in a way that was not possible before.

Determine the real ROI of the system

Now we get to the nitty-gritty. These are the numbers that the CIO and CEO will really be looking for. There's a great deal of nonsense talked about Return on Investment in the technology industry, and there are some very spurious calculations of this magic number, particularly by the larger vendors. Realistically, the only ROI number you can rely on is the one you calculate yourself, based on your own implementation costs and benefits. The calculation itself is as follows:

 Return on investment = annual benefit divided by the investment amount.

So how do we derive these figures? Well coming up with the investment amount shouldn't be a problem for a well governed project. We should have detailed figures of all the costs that we've incurred putting in jBPM: it's simply a matter of totalling them up. Deriving the annual benefit of the new system is a bit more difficult as one can interpret "benefit" in a number of ways. The following is a suggestion for how to calculate annual benefit, but feel free to adapt it to your own situation. Annual benefit is:

Increased revenue: calculated by working out how many more cycles of the process we can now complete per year as a result of implementing the system, multiplied by the average revenue take of a single instance of the process.

Plus:

Reduction in costs: calculated by working out the cost of a single instance of the new process, minus the cost we originally estimated for a single instance of the old process, multiplied by the new number of process cycles per year. Obviously, this is the moment when it pays to have done good quality process metrics analysis on the old process.

It can also sometimes be valid to include some more intangible measures in this calculation of annual benefit. For example, if the implementation of a BPM system has genuinely affected your competitive position, you might say that it has added to the value of your brand. You might also come up with some figures for a reduction in staff turnover because of increased job satisfaction, decreased training costs because the process is now supported, improved customer satisfaction due to a more consistent quality of output, and so on. For the purposes of demonstration, we'll stick with our simple calculation as above:

> Investment amount = taking into account all our labor, hardware, and software costs, our jBPM implementation cost Bland Records $112,000.
>
> Increased revenue = due to the decrease in process turnaround time, we can now complete two more instances of the process per year. Each instance of the process makes on average $200,000, so our increase in revenue is $400,000.
>
> Reduction in costs = due to the automation of some points of the process and the fact that the process is now easier to understand and hence cheaper to staff, we have managed to save 10% of our costs per instance of the process. Our old process used to cost $80,875 per cycle but it now costs just $72,787.50. So if we can now run 14 cycles of the process per year compared to the old 12 our reduction in costs is ($80,875 - $72,787.50) x 14 = $113,225.
>
> Therefore:
>
> Bland Records ROI on their BPM implementation = ($400,000 + $113,225) / $112,000
>
> **ROI = 4.6**

That is an extremely healthy number!

Obtain project sign-off

With big checkmarks next to each of our success criteria and a ROI number that major vendors would shed blood for, it is surely a formality gaining sign-off from Mr Gali that this project is complete. In obtaining sign-off, not only are we formally wrapping up the project, we are also putting the BPM system into "business as usual" mode. This is an important stage, as the system now moves from having a status as an investment for Bland Records, to becoming a cost base. The upshot is that Bland Records can no longer enjoy the tax breaks it did when it was investing in its business. Typically, this means much tighter control over further expenditure and a serious slow down on system change, so we had better be sure we judged our point of go-live correctly. Assuming all is in order, however, we should be able to obtain sign-off from our sponsor to shut down the project.

Process analysis and improvement

The upfront process improvements, systemization, and automation we have already made is really only half the story. Once you have your BPM system integrated into your organization, you have really only scratched the surface of the process benefits you can expect to achieve. Higher quality analysis resulting from real and accurate process metrics can lead to much more important process improvements as time goes on. It may take several years for these improvements to emerge, but an investment in a business process management system is the gift that goes on giving.

Track process metrics

So how do we realize these extraordinary promises? Well, the key starting point is our process metrics. Now that the system is bedded in, and we can see the kind of data that is coming through, we can assess how important the process metrics we chose to track really are. Are we giving our management team the right tools to make business decisions, or are there other KPIs we should be tracking? Luckily, with our SeeWhy business intelligence platform integration, making changes to the process metrics we are tracking is a simple task.

As we build up a history of process execution, we can start to see whether the guesstimates we made for our key performance indicators were on target or not. With the real data in front of us, we can see the minimum, maximum, and average of any of the process metrics we are tracking in SeeWhy. We can use this data to tweak our KPIs to better reflect real life. Realistic KPIs are important because when an exception to the norm occurs, we now know it is a real exception, rather than the stab in the dark effort we had before BPM came along. This means management effort is targeted in the right places and that staff don't feel they are being held accountable for unrealistic targets.

For example, let's imagine that we have decided to use SeeWhy to track the time it takes from when we enter the "Record backing vocals" node to the time we leave it. This will give us the full cycle time for this process activity. Over time, we will build up a good idea of what the "normal" time range is for this activity, allowing us to set up a realistic KPI of, say, one day. Based on this we might decide to set up SeeWhy, so that we are notified if this metric dramatically exceeds this specified KPI: longer than two days for instance. Assuming this notification is sent to the right person, this will allow management to keep on top of anomalies.

Over time, we can also spot trends in our metrics data. Hopefully, these trends will always be in the right direction, but of course there will always be those which go the other way. With hard data available in real time to back up the recognition of these trends, strong management decisions can be made to rectify the situation.

For example, taking the metric we were tracking above, if we configured the SeeWhy metric dimensions correctly, we might notice that certain musicians take longer than others to record their backing vocals. Having spotted this trend we can do something about it and make sure this part of the process is running as fast as possible.

Change request processes

Our jBPM system is now embedded in Bland Records and people are now relying on it to do their day to day jobs. Hence jBPM is now a mission-critical application for Bland Records and must be handled with care. The change process must be designed to ensure only compelling changes are put through, and that the live system is protected from process and code amendments that have been developed too rapidly.

In general terms, the change process that we put together should probably look something like this:

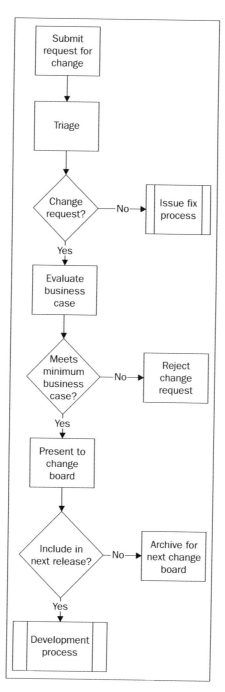

It is important to note that this change request process must be able to handle changes to the underlying business process as well as to jBPM itself. There are considerations to bear in mind for each of these types of change.

Business process changes

As discussed in the previous section, our process metrics have allowed us to build up an excellent cost picture of our process. This is a first-rate springboard from which we can evaluate the suggestions for process change that come through: we can calculate the cost versus the estimated expected benefit of the change. With these figures we can put together a proper business case for our steering committee to base its decision on.

jBPM changes

The change process for jBPM itself should be like that of any mission-critical application. However, it is important to remember that jBPM is subject to ongoing development by the open-source community. The first consideration in this regard is to ensure that your own developments don't take your cut of the jBPM codebase too far from the community's roadmap: doing so would leave you on your own. The second consideration is that if you do develop jBPM along the lines of the jBPM roadmap then you should donate your work back to the community, thus improving the product for everyone, as well as ensuring your developments are supported and built on by the jBPM project.

Business process documentation

With the hurly burly of the development phase out of the way, there is now more time to devote to "nice to have" features of our BPM system. One of these features that we might like to develop further is our online process documentation for our users. Why would we want to do this? Well, an intuitive system is one thing, but the reality of naive users is quite another. In truth, a user community is much more likely to fully adopt a new system if users have crystal clear documentation talking them through what they have to do and why they have to do it. Ideally, this documentation should be available from go-live, if not before to coincide with training, but in the real world this is unlikely to get the resources it needs.

Good quality business process documentation pays for itself. It provides the basis of training materials, which would otherwise be dry and hard to understand without a process context. This means that new hires can be brought in much more easily. Not only will new people benefit, but also our existing staff will work smarter if they understand how their cog fits into the larger machine. With an understanding of how their work affects others in the process chain, our staff are more likely to be motivated to produce quality work.

What kind of documentation?

Traditional process documentation usually consists of Visio files stuck somewhere on a network drive on the off-chance that anyone who takes the trouble to find them might bother to open them up and have a look. If you're really lucky the process diagrams might have been exported as PDFs or as images so that our users who don't have Visio can open them up. These files sit on the network gathering virtual dust and are normally out of date by the time the first person comes across them.

The other scenario is where we have had expensive consultants in, to build us a "knowledge base". This generally looks amazing when it is presented to us, but then we soon start to realize that making changes to it is such an arduous process that no one will ever take the trouble. We might even be locked in and have to phone up the consultants who built it every time we want to change something. The traditional knowledge base is an expensive maintenance nightmare that never fulfils expectations.

Our documentation has to be much smarter than this, we want it to:

- Be comprehensive
- Be simple to understand
- Be easy to navigate
- Be easy to maintain
- Allow users to contribute and feel a sense of ownership

Fortunately, there is a fantastic tool which, when used correctly, can really fit the bill for all these requirements: the wiki.

Using a wiki

For those of you who have not visited planet Earth in the last few years, a wiki is basically a type of website where you can easily edit the web pages. You simply click an "Edit" button, type your changes and then save them: hey, presto! The page is updated. The most famous example is Wikipedia (http://www.wikipedia.org), where people around the world contribute as a community to building an online encyclopedia. We are going to do something very similar with our users. We are going to provide a framework of business process, around which our users are going to collaboratively build up documentation that helps them complete that process.

A wiki is fast to develop, cheap to set up, and cheap to run. There are many flavors of wiki available; lots of them open source, so we don't even have to invest a great deal in the software. You can even download the code that runs Wikipedia, a wiki platform called Mediawiki (http://sourceforge.net/projects/wikipedia), although there are simpler wiki platforms out there for the uninitiated. We will leave it up to the reader to decide which wiki flavor they prefer.

The important thing about a wiki is that it is a collaborative environment. If we set up a sensible editorial policy that allows our users to edit the pages they need without destroying the process framework, we can build a comprehensive and up-to-date set of documentation that will never go stale, and which doesn't have the same barriers to access and maintenance as the more traditional process documentation solutions.

The first step is to build the business process framework from which we will hang off the detailed documentation. The ideal way to do this is to have the home page of our wiki feature a simplified view of our process map diagram. Using simple HTML image maps, we can then allow our users to click through the process steps to get to the next level down in the process hierarchy. Of course, if you can't embed HTML in your wiki, you can always use a simple ordered list of the process steps and link each one through to the next level down.

On the next level down, we want to organize our process information in a consistent manner. The headings you use will depend on your situation, but here is a suggestion for what can work at the process step level:

- Overview: a narrative overview of the activity, how it fits into the context of the process.
- Activity steps: detailed training steps for completing this activity.
- Business rules: any business rules that govern how the activity should be performed.
- Data quality best practice: how do we want users to enter data for this activity?
- KPIs: how do we judge whether the activity has been performed well or not?
- Ownership: who owns this activity?

The ownership question is an important one. There are two kinds of ownership we need to think about here. Who owns this activity from a change process point of view? In other words, who will be asked to sign off if we want to make a change to this activity? And who is the editorial owner for this section of the process documentation? It generally makes sense to nominate one person to keep an eye on a section of the documentation to ensure it is growing in the right way, and to correct editing mistakes as the documentation is built.

The detailed documentation can be linked from underneath each of these sub-headings, so that we build up a documentation hierarchy that looks something like this:

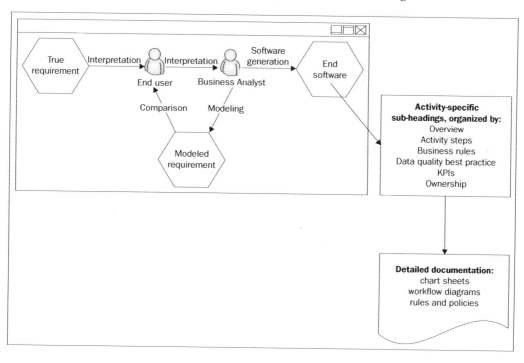

Over time, this business process wiki should build into an invaluable resource that is a real asset for your organization.

Ideas for further development

There are many avenues for further development that could be explored with jBPM: in fact, there are as many variations as there are implementation business scenarios. In this section, we will present a few ideas for taking jBPM further, leaving it up to the reader to decide which are worth further investigation and experimentation.

Breaking up the process into phases using superstates

JBoss jBPM supports the notion of process "superstates", which we can use to split up our long process into process phases. This can be very useful when we want to report on the status of a process instance: rather than having to tie down the instance to a single node, we can report back that the instance is in the "such and such phase".

For example, we might want to break up our "Produce music products" process into four phases, such as:

- Band formation
- Band development
- Album recording
- Album production

In terms of the JPDL syntax we use to achieve this, we define superstate nodes in the same way as any other node. We cannot start or end the process with a superstate, so we must have a start state node that immediately transitions to the next node, using a forward slash to denote that we are descending a level of the hierarchy into a superstate node's collection of nodes. We then use the superstate tags to encapsulate all the nodes that form that phase of the process. When the phase is over, we use "../" to move up a level of the hierarchy, out of that particular superstate and on to the next superstate phase's first node. The JPDL looks like this:

```
<start-state name="Hold auditions">
    <transition name="" to="Band formation/Select band members"></
transition>
    </start-state>
  <super-state name="Band formation">
    <task-node name="Select band members">
        ...
        <transition name="" to="Call SeeWhy"></transition>
    </task-node>

        ... the rest of this phase's task nodes ...

    <task-node name="Name band">
        <transition name="" to="../Band development/Organize vocal
tuition"></transition>
    </task-node>
    </super-state>
    <super-state name="Band development">
    <task-node name="Organize vocal tuition">
        ...
        <transition name="" to="fork1"></transition>
    </task-node>

        ... and so on ...

    </super-state>
        ...
```

As you can see, this is relatively simple JPDL syntax. It must be said, however, that the jBPM Designer diagram view does not support this particularly well in its current incarnation. Hopefully, future versions will find better ways of representing superstates.

Abstracting into a process hierarchy

In a similar vein, if we have a very long process stream, we might want to break up our process into a set of sub-processes that are governed by a single parent process. JPDL supports this through "process composition". A parent process is built from a series of "process state" nodes, each of which represents the complete execution path of a particular sub-process.

Building up a process hierarchy in this way can make the job of process maintenance an easier one. As process definitions are developed and become more complex, working with shorter sub-processes is less cumbersome than working with a long one of labyrinthine complexity. Having said this, connecting all the sub-processes together is not a simple task in the current implementation of JPDL, as you have to map each variable that you want to pass from the current sub-process onto the next by hand. This rather negates the benefit of abstracting the long process into a hierarchy. Hopefully, future incarnations of JPDL will do this a bit more tidily. The current syntax for doing process composition in JPDL is as follows:

```
<process-definition name="Produce music products">
  <start-state>
    <transition to="Sub-process 1 state" />
  </start-state>
  <process-state name="Sub-process 1 state">
    <sub-process name="Sub-process 1" />
    <variable name="1" access="read,write" mapped-name="11" />
    <variable name="2" access="read" mapped-name="22" />
    <transition to="..." />
  </process-state>
  ...
</process-definition>
```

As you can see, this can get rather clunky when lots of variables need to be passed through the hierarchy.

Building a process-driven enterprise

One use of process composition that does make sense is to connect two related but distinct processes together for the purposes of building a single integrated process. For example, now that we have a working process definition for Bland Records' "Produce music products" process, we might consider doing the same thing for the next process along in the hierarchy, namely "Coordinate manufacture". When we have done this, rather than having the two processes run on a standalone basis, we would probably want to connect the two together. We can easily connect the two together with the process composition syntax mentioned above, and there should be fewer variables that require passing across between these two distinct processes than would need to be passed through a sub-divided single process. If we were to perform this exercise for all our business processes, then we would be talking about the Shangri-la of BPM: the fully process-driven enterprise.

Automate business rules processing

Business rules are statements that define or constrain some aspect of the business and therefore govern process execution. We have already implemented some simplistic decision making in our process definition, but this is only the tip of the iceberg. With a little imagination, there are endless scenarios where we can let the system take the strain of making process decisions. Doing this can be a valuable exercise for an organization, as it can mean that:

- Staffing costs are reduced—you don't need such smart people making decisions.
- The quality of output goes up—computers don't make mistakes (much).
- Process throughput is increased—because a computer can perform a decision calculation in a tiny fraction of the time taken by a human.

We have a number of strategies at our disposal for implementing decision making in our BPM system:

- Model a normal task node and have a human perform the decision making.
- Model a decision node and use the inbuilt jBPM expression language to make a decision based on the process variables at hand.
- Model a node that uses an action to call out to an external system that specializes in making complex decisions.

We have already seen how we can use task forms to enable decision making by humans. Let's now see the syntax for making jBPM do the decision making. In order to evaluate a decision, we need to create a decision node and insert an expression that will calculate the outcome of the decision based on the input of whatever process or task variables are appropriate. We specify multiple leaving transitions, each one containing a condition, and jBPM will take the first one that evaluates to true. If none of the transitions specified resolves to true, the first transition listed will be taken, so the first transition should always represent the "otherwise" path. The syntax for a decision node looks like this:

```
<decision name="decision1">
    <transition name="otherwisetransition" to="Otherwise node" condi
tion="#{someVariable > 1}"></transition>
    <transition name="iftruetransition" to="If true node" condition=
"#{someVariable <= 1}"></transition>
  </decision>
```

The expression itself is written in a Java expression language that is used in Java Server Pages and Java Server Faces code. You can find more details of this expression language here:

```
http://java.sun.com/j2ee/1.4/docs/tutorial/doc/JSPIntro7.html
```

As an example, let's see how we could re-implement the "All contracts agreed?" node as a decision node. At the moment, we are using a task form and a human is looking at the state of the bmxAgreed variables to decide whether they all evaluate to "Yes" or not:

```
<task-node name="All contracts agreed?">
    <task name="All contracts agreed" swimlane="Legal adviser">
        <controller>
            <variable name="bm1Agreed" access="read" mapped-name="Band
member 1 agreed?"></variable>
            <variable name="bm2Agreed" access="read" mapped-name="Band
member 2 agreed?"></variable>
            <variable name="bm3Agreed" access="read" mapped-name="Band
member 3 agreed?"></variable>
            <variable name="bm4Agreed" access="read" mapped-name="Band
member 4 agreed?"></variable>
            <variable name="bm5Agreed" access="read" mapped-name="Band
member 5 agreed?"></variable>
            <variable name="bm6Agreed" access="read" mapped-name="Band
member 6 agreed?"></variable>
        </controller>
    </task>
    <transition name="No" to="Contract new member"></transition>
    <transition name="Yes" to="Name band"></transition>
</task-node>
```

To automate this, all we need to do is change the node type to a decision node and include a condition on the transitions that will automatically evaluate whether every *agreed* variable is equal to "Yes" or not:

```
<decision-node name="All contracts agreed?">
    <transition name="No" to="Contract new member" condition="
#{(bm1Agreed=="No") or (bm2Agreed=="No") or (bm3Agreed=="No") or
(bm4Agreed=="No") or (bm5Agreed=="No") or (bm6Agreed=="No")}"></
transition>
    <transition name="Yes" to="Name band" condition="#{(bm1Ag
reed=="Yes") and (bm2Agreed=="Yes") and (bm3Agreed=="Yes") and
(bm4Agreed=="Yes") and (bm5Agreed=="Yes") and (bm6Agreed=="Yes")}"></
transition>
</task-node>
```

Now, if any of the *agreed* variables is a "No", we will take the "No" transition, just as we would if a human had read the variables in a task form.

For more complex decisions, we can build an implementation of the jBPM `DecisionHandler` class to perform the decision calculation. This Java class will then return a transition name to tell jBPM which leaving transition should be taken as a result of the decision.

Quite complex decision making can therefore be done within jBPM itself. However, there are occasions where the business rules that are being evaluated are so complicated that it would be a Herculean task to write the code required to perform the decision making. Indeed, in these scenarios we will probably already have a system that is specifically designed to make these kinds of decisions. In this case, we need to write a state node with multiple leaving transitions, and which has an action on node-enter to call out to the business rules engine system, providing it with any process variables it needs to perform the decision calculation. The state node will then wait until the external system responds with a trigger specifying the leaving transition that should be taken, for instance with code such as `Token.signal(String transitionName)`.

A typical example of where business rules require this kind of heavy-duty processing is in the insurance industry. Our process might collect data off an insurance claim form and put it into process variables, then submit those process variables to a business rules engine, which would respond with a yes or no as to whether the claim is valid and should be paid.

Replace the user information database

We have seen in previous chapters how we have altered the jBPM database tables that contain user information in order to provide login and process role functionality to the web console. While this works well, it does mean we have to maintain our own user database, whereas it probably makes sense to plug directly into our existing company directory that will already have organization information set up in it, for example, Active Directory or an LDAP directory. As this should always be up to date, integrating in this way will remove an administration task from our jBPM workload.

Doing this kind of integration involves ripping out the jBPM identity component. This is not a simple task and is beyond the scope of what we can cover here. For more information on how to do this, please look at the jBPM user guide, wiki, and forums on www.jboss.com.

Document management

One of the most common scenarios in a business process is the handing back and forth of a document. For example, the insurance claim form that we cited above would be passed around numerous departments in the insurance company before a decision was made on the claim. The problem with documents is that they have a tendency to disappear. Even when the document in question is stored electronically, we can still have problems with versioning and controlling access to the document by multiple users.

One way to get around the inherent problems with the use of documents in an organization is to implement some kind of document management system, such as Documentum's Eroom, Microsoft's Sharepoint, or Alfresco's Alfresco ECM. These systems make sure your documents are secure and backed-up, that the right people have access and don't interfere with each other's edits, and that documents are properly versioned. These systems have become an absolute necessity in today's world of co-located teams that work together on projects from multiple global locations.

But why not take this a stage further and integrate your document management system of choice with jBPM? Many of these systems provide the hooks needed to interact with the document store programmatically, so integrating with jBPM is really only a case of writing action handlers that perform the necessary action on the document store. For example, in our insurance claim form scenario above, we might have nodes in our process definition like:

- Receive claim form
- Scan in claim form
- Store claim form

We could then automate the "Store claim form" node by writing an action handler that takes as input a variable that points to the location of our scanned-in file and then copies that file into the document store. The action handler could then return a new process variable that is a pointer to the document's location in the document store, so later nodes in the process can also interact with the document. As this would be a relatively advanced integration, we'll leave it up to the reader to pursue.

Summary

So we are finished: it is time to put our feet up and reap the bounteous rewards of all our hard work. We have put together a full-featured and complete business process management system that meets the expectations of the people involved and provides real value to the client business. This is an investment that will go on paying back in the years to come, with incremental process improvements being identified and implemented. There are rich opportunities for further development of our system, bringing increased process automation, and a smoother execution of the process.

I hope this book has given you the tools you need to put together a successful business process management system implementation project and I wish you the very best of luck in your BPM endeavors.

Epilogue

Flushed with success and awash with spare cash, Sven Gali decided to expand his business beyond the narrow confines of the record industry. He created spin-off companies in diverse industries, all under the "Bland" banner. The Bland combined circus and airline service was a huge hit, as was the rope recycling venture. Sadly Bland's range of Indian foods was not so successful. With a vast fortune amassed, Mr Gali turned away from the business world, dabbling in extreme sports and record-breaking adventures. He became the first man to successfully single-handedly cross the Atlantic in a coracle and narrowly failed to beat the world record for "holding one's breath".

Gali has since been awarded a knighthood in the Queen's millennium New Year's honours list for "services to entrepreneurship".

Index

user information database, replacing 200
process, improving
  process metrics, tracking 190
  request process, changing 190, 192
process changes
  business process changes 192
  jBPM changes 192
  requesting 190-192
process forecasting 160
process management 159
process metrics analysis 159
process monitoring. *See* **BAM**
process reporting suite
  about 160
  SeeWhy Business Intelligence platform,
    integrating 160
project, assessing
  about 185
  evaluating 186
  project post mortem 186
  ROI, determining 188
project, setting up
  business scenario 23
  initiation document 24, 25
  kick off meeting 34
  scope, deciding 25-28
  team, forming 29-34
project initiation document
  about 24
  high level project plan 24
  project objective, identifying 24
  success criteria, identifying 24
  uses 24
project team
  forming 29
  process owners 31, 32
  project office 30
  project sponsors, identifying 30
  subject matter experts 31, 32
proof of concept
  expectations, setting up 128
  jBPM, making available on server 130-132
  planning 129
  requirements, capturing 129, 130
  running 132
  setting up 127
  team, setting up 127, 128

prototype, iterating
  about 132
  process changes 132
  system, integrating 134-140
  task, priotarizing 133
prototype user interface
  building 99
  deploying 114, 115
  developing 100-106
  iterating 132
  process, deploying 114, 115
  users, setting up 106-113

Q

quick wins
  identifying 48
  keywords 48

R

RACI matrix
  about 42
  process, evaluating 44
  process, putting along side 44
  rules 42
rapid implementation projects
  identifying 48
responsibilities
  identifying 38
Return on Invesment. *See* **ROI**
ROI
  determining 188, 189
  increased revenue 188
  reduction in costs 188
roles
  identifying 38

S

scope of project
  about 25
  process 26
  process, defining 26
  process hierarchy 27
SeeWhy
  about 160
  action handler code 166, 167

BAM, using for 182
BAM points, setting up on graph 164-166
data, interpreting 173-176
email notifications, setting up 178-181
event interface, configuring 170-173
features 177, 178
getting 162
installing 162, 163
jBPM JBoss server, configuring 168
process event 168, 169
software development
BPM approach, using 6
software development, BPM
Agile methodology 7
methodologies 6-9
project life cycle 15
waterfall approach 6
waterfall approach, disadvantages 6
success criteria
about 186
swimlanes
adding 80

T

team. *See* **project team**

U

user interface
building 99
prototype, building 99
prototype, developing 100
users
setting up 106

W

web console interface
about 116
adapting 124, 125
end users 119-121
managers 122
working with 116-118
wiki
about 193
documentation, creating 193-195
workflow
mapping 35
mapping, flowchart technique used 35
notations 36
process mapping tools 36

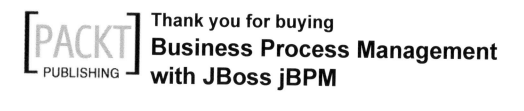
Thank you for buying
Business Process Management with JBoss jBPM

Packt Open Source Project Royalties

When we sell a book written on an Open Source project, we pay a royalty directly to that project. Therefore by purchasing Business Process Management with JBoss jBPM, Packt will have given some of the money received to the JBoss jBPM project.

In the long term, we see ourselves and you—customers and readers of our books—as part of the Open Source ecosystem, providing sustainable revenue for the projects we publish on. Our aim at Packt is to establish publishing royalties as an essential part of the service and support a business model that sustains Open Source.

If you're working with an Open Source project that you would like us to publish on, and subsequently pay royalties to, please get in touch with us.

Writing for Packt

We welcome all inquiries from people who are interested in authoring. Book proposals should be sent to authors@packtpub.com. If your book idea is still at an early stage and you would like to discuss it first before writing a formal book proposal, contact us; one of our commissioning editors will get in touch with you.

We're not just looking for published authors; if you have strong technical skills but no writing experience, our experienced editors can help you develop a writing career, or simply get some additional reward for your expertise.

About Packt Publishing

Packt, pronounced 'packed', published its first book "Mastering phpMyAdmin for Effective MySQL Management" in April 2004 and subsequently continued to specialize in publishing highly focused books on specific technologies and solutions.

Our books and publications share the experiences of your fellow IT professionals in adapting and customizing today's systems, applications, and frameworks. Our solution-based books give you the knowledge and power to customize the software and technologies you're using to get the job done. Packt books are more specific and less general than the IT books you have seen in the past. Our unique business model allows us to bring you more focused information, giving you more of what you need to know, and less of what you don't.

Packt is a modern, yet unique publishing company, which focuses on producing quality, cutting-edge books for communities of developers, administrators, and newbies alike. For more information, please visit our website: www.PacktPub.com.

Implementing SugarCRM

ISBN: 1-904811-68-X   Paperback: 328 pages

A step-by-step guide to using this powerful Open Source application in your business.

1. Your complete guide to SugarCRM implementation – assess your needs, install the software, start using it, train users, integrate with existing systems

2. Covers both the free and commercial versions of SugarCRM – get maximum benefit from the free version before paying for add ons

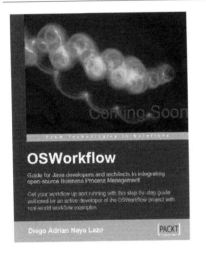

OSWorkflow

ISBN: 978-1-847191-52-6   Paperback: 200 pages

Get your workflow up and running with this step-by-step guide authored by an active developer of the OSWorkflow project with real-world examples

1. Basics of OSWorkflow

2. Integrating business rules with Drools

3. Task scheduling with Quartz

Please check **www.PacktPub.com** for information on our titles

3320283